The Everyday Enneagram

The Everyday Enneagram

*A Personality Map for
Enhancing Your Work, Love,
and Life . . . Every Day*

by Lynette Sheppard

NINE POINTS PRESS
PETALUMA, CALIFORNIA

Although the author and publisher have made every effort to ensure the accuracy and completeness of information contained in this book, we assume no responsibility for errors, inaccuracies, omissions, or any inconsistency herein. Any slights of people, places, or organizations are unintentional.

Cover photo by Dewitt Jones. © Dewitt Jones Productions, Inc.

First printing 2000

ISBN 0-9700240-5-3

LCCN 00-132897

ATTENTION CORPORATIONS, UNIVERSITIES, COLLEGES, AND PROFESSIONAL ORGANIZATIONS: Quantity discounts are available on bulk purchases of this book for educational purposes. Special books or book excerpts can also be created to fit specific needs. For information, please contact Nine Points Press, 11 La Cresta Drive, Petaluma, CA 94952.

To the love of my life, Dewitt,
and to son Brian and daughter Deanna,
all of whom continue to teach me the value
of the Enneagram—every day.

ACKNOWLEDGMENTS

I will be forever grateful to Cathie Haynes for bringing the Enneagram into my life and for her discerning counsel regarding this book. I also owe a debt of gratitude to my teachers Helen Palmer and David Daniels, whose work with the Oral Tradition™ and panels of exemplars representing the nine types continues to inspire and inform my own work.

I also wish to thank Charles Miller and Nancy Stetson for believing in this project and for editorial guidance, Bronwyn Cooke for artistic expertise, Louise Cochran for ideas and "happy thoughts," Maggie Bedrosian and Susan Bradley for manuscript suggestions and cheerleading, and Sam Horn for invaluable help and advice.

Most of all, I am indebted to those who have so willingly shared their inner landscapes. This book could never have been written without their stories and insights on using the Enneagram in everyday life.

TABLE OF CONTENTS

Discovering the Map

Fifteen years ago I went to lunch with my good friend, Cathie, at least once a week. Often she would delight in some mannerism or verbalization of mine, proclaiming, "Oh, you are such a Seven!" Annoyed yet intrigued, I promised to learn about the Enneagram (pronounced any-uh-gram) if she would quit describing me in numbers. It turned out to be one of the best decisions of my life.

For the first time, I began to understand some of the patterns that ruled my life seemingly without my volition. With this knowledge came a newfound freedom—I might not have to repeat the same mistakes over and over again. I also found a "map" for my gifts and how to maximize them. I began to see how others might experience me, both positively and negatively.

What was equally important, I began to learn about the internal motivations and worldviews of those closest to me, finding that my way of seeing the world was only one right answer. There were eight other dramatically different ways of seeing and being in the world. And they were as right as mine! Learning the Enneagram gave me a chance to begin to experience how these other eight "types" felt inside. I'd learned a number of personality systems that shed light on various behaviors and characteristics. But until the Enneagram, I'd never had a map for how it felt to be inside another's skin, looking out from their eyes.

The Enneagram changed my perceptions about myself and others. I became more aware of my impact on people. I learned my habitual or

1

automatic way of looking at situations and began to examine my assumptions. I questioned my particular version of reality and found a
way to break the patterns that did not serve me.

In using the Enneagram with others, I discovered new depth in
relationships. I learned more about the inner world of my spouse and
children. New understanding strengthened and deepened our connections. I'm still learning from them!

I won't say that my life has been made easier by the Enneagram,
though I can certainly point to instances where it has helped smooth
the way. Staying awake to and noticing my personality's automatic mode
isn't always easy. Yet my life and relationships have been made much
fuller and richer. I work better. I love better. And I live better. I couldn't
ask for anything more.

How This Book Came to Be

My students reported, "I've gained a lot of insight into myself (or
my boss, my kids, my spouse, my parents, etc.) through the Enneagram.
I've really enjoyed learning about the nine personality types. But I still
don't know how to use the Enneagram on a day-to-day basis."

This quandary was expressed by most of my students, even those
who had completed advanced work. I gave out exercises to some, ideas
and homework to others. I passed on how others had used the Enneagram
in their lives. However it was piecemeal and something was missing.
Insight might have been interesting, but something more was needed.

The Enneagram's greatest benefit is that it is a practical tool for
dealing with self and others on a daily basis. This book began as a manual
for my students and evolved into a guide for actually putting to use the
compelling information offered by the Enneagram.

How to Use This Book

This book is not meant to be read in a linear fashion, from front to
back. Those new to the Enneagram will want to read chapters 1 and 2
to begin to find their own types. Once one knows one's type, the system offers a number of practical applications in everyday life. Then
skip around to the chapter that most meets your needs at the present
time. If you are having difficulty with a particular person in your work
life, go directly to Chapter 8 for exercises and ideas. If you are wonder-

ing how to relate better to your children, read Chapter 7 first. If intimate relationships are your foremost concern, do not pass GO, do not collect $200, skip to Chapter 6. If you are most interested in your own personal growth, Chapter 5 is your first stop. And if interest in the Enneagram as an adjunct to spiritual life is your primary interest, by all means visit Chapter 9.

Use this as a workbook. When faced with a problem or question in a particular life area, peruse the chapter focusing on that subject. Visit the chapters as needed. Perform the exercises, note what works and what doesn't. Develop your own ways of working with the Enneagram.

If you get stuck or have questions, visit my Web site at www.9points.com. The Gathering Place Bulletin Board hosted there is a resource for the worldwide Enneagram community. In the Oral Tradition™ Enneagram as I learned it from Helen Palmer and David Daniels, the best source for information about a particular Enneagram type or "point" was someone who inhabited that point. In other words, if you are having questions about how to deal with a Nine, ask another Nine. An Enneagram teacher can help by knowing all nine perspectives. But unless she is a Nine, she won't really know what it is like to live there. Only another Nine really knows. On the Bulletin Board at 9points.com, you can ask questions of people in each of the nine types.

Feel welcome to tell your own story. Enneagram knowledge is best passed on by all of us telling our stories and sharing our insights about what works and what does not. If you have an Enneagram story to share, email me at Lynette@everydayenneagram.com.

A Map, Not the Territory

There are many maps that can help us relate better to others or allow us to become our best selves. The Enneagram is only one of these. I believe it is one of the best, since it describes the *motivations and worldview* underlying behavior and traits, rather than enumerating characteristics alone. Yet the Enneagram too has limitations. It is only a map, a guide. It *cannot* completely reflect the territory it describes. As long as it contributes to understanding, compassion, and growth, it is a useful map. When it becomes entrenched as reality or truth, it has become a barrier to that same understanding. Use it, but hold it lightly as with any model or map. New cartographers may update our maps at any time. I look forward to the day when we are so open and connected we will no longer need any map to understand ourselves and one another. Until that day comes, the Enneagram can help illuminate the intrinsic beauty in each one of us.

Deadly sins

1 = anger
2 = pride
3 = deceit appearance over substance
4 = envy : they are missing something
5 = avarice - hoard things
* 6 - fear - worst case scenarios
     hold-back love & affection
7 - gluttony - gorge on positive exp.
   "never statisfied".
8 - lust - confrontational
9 - sloth - fell asleep to needs of own self.
- 7 = are addicted.
   I don't want to feel -

* more 6's in America -

The Road Back to You.
   Ian Morgan -
   Cron - Crohn.

CHAPTER 1

The Enneagram– What Is It and How Can It Help Me?

The Enneagram is a map of our internal terrain, of personality and human potential. Like other maps of personality, such as the Myers-Briggs, it describes how we appear to others—our external terrain. This external aspect of our personality is comprised of traits, actions and reactions, coping methods, speaking styles, ways of assimilating infor-

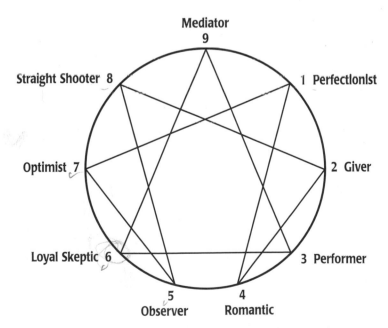

Figure 1-1 *The Enneagram—map of the internal terrain*

5

mation, etc. A "mapping" of personality's external terrain gives us valuable information furthering our quest to better understand ourselves and others. What is unique about the Enneagram and makes it so powerful a tool for everyday life is that this system also maps our internal terrain: what drives us, our general worldview (understanding of the world and what life is about) and how it feels to be us, from the inside.

Who's Running the Show?

The Enneagram map describes nine basic personality types or worldviews. Each of the types or "points" (referring to their position on the Enneagram diagram) has a specific gift or attribute that contributes to the full spectrum of human potential. Each attribute has a "high side" and a "low side." The high side reflects the optimal expression of our personality's gift. The low side results when we are adversely driven by our personality under conditions of stress or difficulty and can lead to a distortion of our gift. Most of us unconsciously exhibit a combination of both the high and low sides of our personality.

What might it be like if we were conscious or aware of the drive behind our gift? The Enneagram can be a map to conscious participation in our personality's expression. In other words, when we are unaware, our personality runs us. Have you ever asked yourself, "Why is this happening to me again?" "Why does this same pattern occur over and over in my life?" When we know our type, our habitual way of perceiving, feeling, and acting, we find we have choices in our responses. We can choose how to perceive or respond to a situation. The personality no longer runs us; we run it.

Different Maps for Different Chaps

The primary purpose of a map is to establish where we are and to plot the best route to where we are going. Different individuals viewing the same map might have very different beliefs about what constitutes the best route. If efficacy is your desire, then the interstates would seem the best way to travel. If sightseeing is your bent, the blue highways might appear to be the perfect route. Most important in using any map, including the Enneagram map of personality, is that you make it your own. Use it for your individual needs in traveling your life.

Even simple travel maps are seen differently by different readers. As a member of an automobile club, my father would obtain flip-through maps that delineated our family trips into small manageable segments. A wealth of information was contained in these small maplets. Interestingly enough, each of us used the map in a way that suited his or her requirements, focusing on what was most useful and important to us at that particular time.

My mother was concerned with basic needs. She read ahead to find the roadside rest stops, reasoning that preplanned stops would be quicker than finding a service station, getting a key, and so forth, and would get us on our way with the least disruption. For her, it was a comfort station/family harmony map. I looked for points-of-interest, not so concerned about the destination as breaking it up with enjoyable stops at historical sites and such. For me, it was a see-new-things map.

Dad drove and looked for gas stations, restaurants, and lodging spots. Dad was reading a caretaking and security map. My studious younger brother liked to read the notes about each section of countryside we were passing through—what kind of crops grew there, for what the area was known. For him it was a geography lesson. The same map, yet each of us was using it in a way that was most helpful to us in our concerns on the journey. It was as if there were many maps in one.

The Enneagram, too, is actually a number of maps, depending on your specific needs or interests. This book is designed so you can flip to the specific map(s) that will be most useful to you in your everyday life at the present time. How each person internalizes or uses the map will be highly individual.

The first three chapters are map reading courses, designed to acquaint you with your type or point (where you are) and the other eight types, which are places you will visit when you interact with others. If you are already familiar with your type, you can skip ahead to the "Now that I know my type, what do I do with it?" part of the book, beginning with Chapter 4. These subsequent chapters delineate areas in everyday life where a specific Enneagram map can be used to enhance our life's journey.

So Many Maps—So Little Time

The Enneagram map is viewed in a multitude of ways depending on what is most crucial to us at any particular time. You may decide to work with one map at a time, or many simultaneously. Read on to find which areas are most compelling to you.

Self-Actualization

Where am I now? Where am I going? How can I get there? Why do I repeat the same patterns over and over? And then, how can I develop my full potential, get out of my own way, realize my gifts?

The Enneagram provides a map for our self-development, for reaching our greatest potential. As we become conscious of our personality type and the drive that motivate us, we find we have new choices in how we perceive, act, and feel in the world. Our worldview becomes less limited, and we are able to access our high side more often. We can convert our pitfalls into gifts, and learn compassion and understanding for ourselves.

So the Enneagram becomes a map for finding your own gift—the treasure encoded in your personality.

Understanding Others

The Enneagram provides a series of useful maps for understanding and getting along with other people. We learn the external map of their attributes and traits. Yet attributes and even gifts do not make up the most significant aspects of relating to others through the Enneagram. We cannot promote understanding by a simple enumeration of observable traits but must enter the prevailing worldview on the inside. The Enneagram gives us a glimpse into the internal terrain of all nine types. True understanding and compassion follow naturally when we are privy to another's inner territory. External behavior makes sense in this context. Best of all, we don't take that behavior personally. The internal map gives us a hint of the real power of the Enneagram—to see the world through another's eyes.

Whether we are most interested in gaining understanding of others in our intimate relationships, in work and business settings, or in family dynamics, the Enneagram offers us the opportunity of knowing another as he is to himself. We have the privilege, albeit momentarily, to feel what it feels like inside another person's skin.

Intimacy

"I just don't understand why he does that." "No matter what I do, I can't seem to figure her out." "Sometimes I really do believe men are from Mars and women are from Venus!"

One of the most rewarding and challenging of life's journeys is that of intimate relationships. The Enneagram personality system can be at its most powerful when applied to those closest to us. True understanding begins when we can experience the worldview of others in our lives by feeling what reality feels like to them. By leaving our own personality's worldview and shifting our vantage point to our significant other's, we can begin to find ways of dramatically improving our relationships. Intimate relating with another personality type is like visiting another culture. In order to work and love well while in this culture, we need to learn the language and customs. In this way, we can begin to honor one another's unique differences and celebrate our human diversity.

Business Relationships

Do we need to learn the inner landscape of our clients to better honor them and their needs? Or do we need to work on a relationship with a boss or subordinate who does not react the same as we do? Are we responsible for knowing our company's corporate identity and culture to help with visioning and growing or to anticipate and intervene in times of change and turmoil? Are we part of a project team? Any way we look at it, business is about relationships. Productivity is directly related to the quality of relationships we have with our clients, our superiors and employees, and the other contributors on our teams. The Enneagram gives us a map for honoring personal diversity and creating sustainable working relationships with clients and coworkers.

Family Dynamics

A family is a small intentional community. How do we begin to understand and honor our children for whom they are to themselves? The Enneagram can be a great map to family unity, honoring each member. It offers a language for discussing behavior in a nonjudgmental, open fashion. It empowers young people to voice their concerns and feelings, knowing they are not alone or "weird." Children become full members of the community when they can discuss their parents and themselves as people on the Enneagram map—not bad or good, just different. Parents can begin to acknowledge their offsprings' gifts at an early age, promoting higher self-esteem and expression of those gifts. Parents will be less inclined to try to mold their children into replicas of themselves if there is an understanding of their offsprings' worldviews and inherent gifts.

Higher Consciousness

The Enneagram map describes a spiritual path or roadway. The key to our higher self—our essence—lies within the particular gift of our personality. However, this gift gets slightly distorted in our unconscious state, where we are unaware of our essence. Remembering our true Self, via the clues offered by the small personality self, allows us to integrate our spiritual and earthly lives together. This integration can lead to more meaning, joy, and fulfillment, recapturing the sacred in everyday life.

Where Do I Go from Here? How to Use This Book

That's up to you. Are you anxious to figure out your type? Or someone else's? Read ahead to chapters 2 and 3 on the nine types and their corresponding energies. Do you already know your type and want to get down to the practical, how-to-use-every-day information? Skip to the chapter topic that elucidates the Enneagram map most helpful to you: self-development, intimate relationships, business and work, family dynamics, or spirituality. Are you interested in some of the more general information on the Enneagram? Continue on to the FAQs section below.

FAQs (Frequently Asked Questions) About the Enneagram

Why should I learn about my Enneagram point or type? How can it help me?

The short answer: Knowledge of your Enneagram type can make you happier and more fulfilled in your life. *How?* As we learn about our automatic or habitual way of perceiving the world, we can *choose* whether to act or react in the same ways we always have. Learning our type opens us up to more choices. We move from unconscious behavior to conscious behavior. We run our personality, rather than it running us. Our personality's greatest gift can paradoxically be our largest stumbling block if we are not aware of it. Awareness of our Enneagram type can be the first step toward actualizing our full potential, to becoming our best selves.

How do I figure out my own type?

After learning the basics of the nine Enneagram types, self-observation is a must. Observing where attention migrates automatically as well as the slant of your worldview will help you find your type. Books are helpful and many people find their type through reading and subsequent self-observation. If you are still puzzled, attending an introductory class can help, since the energy of each type can be observed and felt. Still confused? A certified Enneagram teacher in the Oral Tradition™ in your area can conduct a "typing interview" to help you with the process of ascertaining your own worldview.

Enneagram tests or inventories are only useful in helping you begin the process of self-observation. They are *not* useful in determining your type. We are just too complicated to be reduced to paper and pencil. I wish they worked—it would be so much easier for each of us to find our type. Then we could begin working with our habitual pattern or personality right away. I've tried all the tests, as have my students and colleagues. They often narrow the search to three to five types that we may access (see Chapter 4).

Yet it is important that we discover our "core" or true type in order to find out how to work effectively with it. Otherwise, we may find ourselves barking up the wrong banyan! Working with a type that is not our true type may indeed teach us something about ourselves as humans, but it will not address the real issues of our personality, nor will it illuminate our specific gifts and foibles. Again, ongoing self-observation is the key to unlocking our true type.

How does it help me to know the other points on the Enneagram?

The Enneagram describes nine *dramatically different* ways of perceiving reality. All nine ways work—no one way is better than another. As we learn the nine unique worldviews, we realize that "objective reality" is the ultimate oxymoron. We no longer limit ourselves to a single perception as we begin to experience others as they are to themselves and see the beauty and perfection of each of the types. Our relationships improve by leaps and bounds when we begin to listen carefully for a tune other than our own. The Enneagram gives us a map for honoring, valuing, and experiencing human diversity.

How do I determine someone else's type?

This is trickier, because we don't necessarily know another person's internal terrain if they have not shared it with us. However, the Enneagram map helps us know what questions to ask another to elicit their internal viewpoint. It matters less that you get their type right than that you open inquiry. A positive byproduct of trying to figure out another's point on the Enneagram is that we listen more carefully. We have an ulterior motive: We want to figure out their type. But an unintended consequence is often that the other senses your genuine interest in them and feels heard. That opens the way for genuine connection.

Aren't we likely to start putting people in boxes or pigeon-holing them into categories with the Enneagram?

It's possible and surely has happened. Any map, even a good one, can be used superficially. (It would be foolish to assume we know Indiana just from reading a road map of the state.) We all categorize every day: man/woman; Hispanic/Asian; small/large; quick/slow; athletic/sedentary. Categories are our way of making sense and order out of our world. Yet we must hold these categorizations loosely, seeing them for the very incomplete picture they are. So it is with the Enneagram, where we look beyond a type to the multifaceted uniqueness of the individual.

Oddly enough, we are already in a box when we are not aware of the ways in which our personality runs or controls us. My spouse speaks to corporations, telling them that "patterns too long unquestioned can become our prisons." Our personality is a pattern of habitual thoughts, feelings, and behaviors. Don't let it become a prison! The Enneagram can help you learn about your pattern. Then you can begin to question it, shift it, shake things up. You can be in control of your personality rather than allow your personality to be in control of you.

What constitutes other difficulties or misuses of the Enneagram?

The Enneagram can be misused in the same way that any system or map can be misused. We can *confuse the map with the territory*, believing that we know all there is to know about someone when we only know their Enneagram type. If we believe that a complex, multifaceted human being can be reduced to this Enneagram point, we miss the opportunity to experience his uniqueness. A person is so much more than her Enneagram type, just as she is more than her gender, political leanings, religious preference, or education level.

Using the Enneagram as a *quick fix* or as a "parlor game" is another possible misuse. Although one can use the Enneagram as soon as one has learned it in even a cursory manner, the true power of the system is that it provides a method of questioning to elicit another person's beliefs, feelings, and worldview. It provides us a non–emotionally charged way to learn about another human being's internal terrain, as well as the uncharted areas of our own inner landscape. However, it has been my experience that those who use the Enneagram superficially generally move on to the next "in" thing and don't really misuse it for any appreciable length of time.

The Enneagram is a system of compassion. It is a misuse to *use it to judge another rather than to understand* him or her. Rather, it allows us to focus on our differences in the true spirit of curiosity, to learn what the world looks like to another. As we learn more about each Enneagram type and its inherent worldview, we begin to understand how others experience themselves and their environments. We find that *all* the types work just fine. Each point has a gift and a set of foibles related to the misuse or distortion of the gift. Awareness of the nine Enneagram types helps us see the beauty in each one of us, even when someone else's worldview is in temporary conflict with our own view of reality.

Awareness of our Enneagram type awakens us to other modes of acting and reacting besides our own personality's modus operandi. We can expand our repertoire for experiencing the world by learning how the other eight types experience it. It is a mistake to *use the Enneagram as a justification for not growing,* for not changing, for remaining fixed and immutable in your personality's position. "I can't help it, I'm a Five (or a Four, a One, a Seven, etc.)" is a poor excuse for any behavior. It is possible that we cannot help our habitual patterns when we are unaware of them, but once we are clued in to the personality and how it functions, we cannot use the knowledge of our Enneagram type as a way to stay locked in it. The Enneagram is a way out of our habits and old patterns, not a pretext for justifying them.

Does your Enneagram type or point ever change? Can you be more than one type?

No. Although you may access any or all of the traits of the various Enneagram types throughout your lifetime, the "default" worldview does not change. When we temporarily lose our awareness or "go unconscious" we revert back to our default position, our home base, our Enneagram type.

Where did our Enneagram point or type originate? Was it determined environmentally or were we born with it?

Presumably, at birth we had all nine types equally present in us. A combination of genetic predisposition and environmental influences caused us to prefer one of the types as our primary way of dealing with the world. Our Enneagram type constituted a way of protecting our childhood vulnerability. Of course, over time the same worldview that protected us as children might get in our way as adults. It is then that our unconscious, habitual way of perceiving and acting impedes our growth and development in later life.

Where did the map come from?

The Enneagram diagram has been traced back approximately 10,000 years. It is said to have been used by Pythagoras to explain the workings of the universe. However, we really know little about its early use. The Sufis used it as a path to higher spiritual growth in their secret societies. Gurdjieff, a Russian mystic, is believed to have learned the Enneagram from a Sufi sect before bringing it to the Western world in the 1940s. Gurdjieff incorporated the Enneagram into his "Fourth Way" teachings. It was purely passed on as an oral tradition from master to student. A hallmark of the teaching stated that each personality type had a chief feature (what we now refer to as the passion, habit, or drive). Gurdjieff worked with his students one-on-one in taming their chief feature. He used movement and dance around the Enneagram diagram as a tool of transformation. But to the best of our knowledge, he did not share the entirety of the Enneagram with his students.

In the early 1970s, a psychologist named Oscar Ichazo figured out the proper placement of the types on the diagram. He taught a select group in Chile his version of the Enneagram. One of those students, Claudio Naranjo, correlated the esoteric information with modern psychological thought and the current version of the Enneagram was born.

Helen Palmer made a significant contribution to the system with the elucidation of the attentional stances of each type. It is much easier to observe how we pay attention, what grabs our attention habitually, and discover our type than it is to "know" our drive, habit, or passion. She promulgated the Oral Tradition™ Enneagram, deriving information about the types by interviewing panels of each type. She felt that the true experts on a particular Enneagram type were the people who inhabit the type. Many others have made significant contributions to the Enneagram: Don Riso and Russ Hudson, Richard Rohr, Tom Condon, Hameed Ali, Margaret Frings Keyes, Patrick O' Leary, Maria Beesing, Elizabeth Wagele, Renee Baron, Theodorre Donson and Kathy Hurley, Michael Goldberg, Anthony Blake, to name a few. The Enneagram continues to grow as we learn more about the internal terrain of the nine personality types it describes.

How do we know there are nine types? Why aren't there five, or ten?

Dr. Belinda Brent, a psychologist, asked herself that very question after studying the Enneagram. She set out to disprove that there were only nine personality types and conducted a study of several thousand people to ascertain their focus of attention. Her findings indicated there were indeed nine distinct attentional stances or personality types. She has since developed a tool to identify those stances called the Brent Attentional Style Inventory (BASI).

Why is the description of the types so negative?

Indeed, the majority of students who've already read descriptions of the nine types pose this question when attending one of my introductory Enneagram classes. It seems all that the books focus on is the flaws or downside of the personality. The gifts are left until the end of the type descriptions, if they are mentioned at all.

In response to this feedback, I attempted to teach a few classes focusing on the strengths and gifts of each point. I was met with blank faces as I enumerated the positive aspects of each of the nine Enneagram types. Once I began sharing the pitfalls and problems of each type, the students came alive. They only discovered their type when they heard the downsides. (Regardless of which type a student was, all nine types responded in this same way.)

Perhaps it is human nature, perhaps it is cultural, but we don't recognize our internal terrain from a listing of our gifts and strengths. We first recognize ourselves by our failings. Our internal terrain, as perceived by ourselves, seems to be defined by our flaws. Maybe it is negative so we can find ourselves. Maybe we want to know what can be shifted or changed when we are no longer run by our personality. Once we find our type, however, it is important we notice and appreciate our innate gifts, as well as the gifts of the other nine types.

What is a "wing"?

Each point also accesses some of the attributes of one or both of the two points next to it on the Enneagram diagram. For example, a Seven may have a Six wing or an Eight wing. While they will still have primarily Seven views and behaviors, their personality will be flavored by Six or Eight. A Seven with the energy of a Six wing will look quite different from a Seven with an Eight wing. Most people have one wing point that is dominant, although at some time in their life they may access the energy of the other wing point. Others are "bi-winged" and access both wing points equally.

Explain movement on the Enneagram to the "stress point."

Our initial response to stress is to "stomp" on our point. We pump up the volume of our normal coping mechanisms and we seem to exaggerate the attributes of our personality type. If this is not successful in relieving stress or anxiety, we "move" on the diagram and

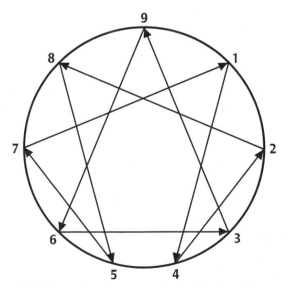

Figure 1-2 *Movement on Enneagram in the direction of stress points.*

access traits of another point. This allows us to take action or alleviate the stress. Stress points are not "bad," they help us. However, as with our Enneagram type, we may access the less desirable aspects of our stress point when we are unconscious of them. As we become more conscious, we may find ourselves utilizing more of the gifts of our stress point and less of the downside. Again, through awareness, we run the stress point of our personality rather than it running us. (See Figure 1-2 and follow the arrows to the stress point for each type. For example, the arrow from One goes to the Four point. So under stress, a One would experience aspects of Four. A Four would experience aspects of Two, and so on.)

Explain movement on the Enneagram to the "security point."

When we are secure, we move to our security point (see Figure 1-3). Often we take on the more positive, beneficial traits of our security point as we grow and evolve. It is possible to experience the low side of your security point as it is possible to experience the high side of your stress point. For any of the energies we access, awareness is the key to full realization of its attendant gifts and strengths.

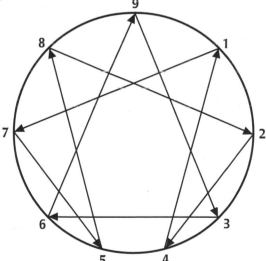

Figure 1-3 *Movement on the Enneagram in the direction of security points.*

If you are a newcomer to the Enneagram, read on and discover your type in the next chapter. If you know your type, you may wish to skip ahead to the map most helpful to you. If you are not conversant with the energy aspect of the Enneagram, you may wish to read Chapter 3 before moving on. This is a fundamental element in understanding and typing others. Working with the energy of the Enneagram also gives us a nonverbal way of approaching and honoring those that inhabit the nine types of the Enneagram.

 # Overview
of the
Nine Types

Each of the Enneagram types has a unique gift that it contributes to the full spectrum of human potential. However, each gift also has a dark side. Much like the yin-yang symbol, with a little spot of light in the dark half and a little spot of dark in the light half, there is a little shadow in each Enneagram type's gift and a little gift in each shadow. We do well to remember here that gifts, characteristics, and traits do not make up the most significant aspect of the Enneagram. We cannot understand ourselves or others by a simple enumeration of observable traits, but instead must enter the prevailing worldview and the beliefs that flower from its seed.

Anyone may exhibit any of the traits of the nine Enneagram types, given the right set of circumstances. For example, confrontation is a trait associated with type Eight. However, being confrontational does not mean we *are* an Eight. Ones are concerned with right and wrong; yet we are not necessarily Ones because we are concerned at times with right vs. wrong.

What defines the types is that which is *underneath* the traits and characteristics that we notice from the outside. The unique worldview, unconscious drive, and beliefs systems of each type are the support structure for the personality or Enneagram type. They make up the internal terrain or inner landscape for each of the nine types or points and give us our first glimpse of the real power of the Enneagram—to open ourselves to new perspectives and see the world through new eyes.

In the following descriptions of the nine points, we will examine the worldview of each type, the underlying premise that informs life and reality as each sees it. We'll look at the beliefs that spring from this view of reality, the unconscious motivational drive, and the focus of attention. An accompanying list of characteristics and traits will make more sense after we consider the worldview. We'll then examine the gift of each type as well as the dark side of the gift—in other words, we'll look at the upside and downside of each Enneagram point. Most importantly, we will get a glimpse of the internal terrain of each type, augmented by a hallmark or defining characteristic, plus an exemplar in their own words.

Type One—the Perfectionist

Worldview
Life is about correcting error and striving for improvement.

Beliefs
Virtue is its own reward. People are their principles and ideals. It's important to be dependable, responsible, and have integrity. Work supersedes pleasure. It would be a better world if we all did our very best and worked to be all that we could be.

Unconscious Drive
Internalized anger—resentment

Focus of Attention
What is right or wrong

Characteristics
- Compulsive need to act on what seems correct
- One right way, black-and-white thinking
- Relentless stream of self-criticizing thoughts
- Mentally comparing oneself to others and concern about criticism
- Belief in one's own moral and ethical superiority
- Procrastination stemming from fear of making a mistake
- Do-gooder—do what *should* be done rather than what one wants to do
- Trapdoor phenomenon—pleasure escape valve

• Scorched earth policy—scrap whole project and start over if even one small part is wrong

Gift

Discernment—Perfectionists have an innate ability to assess potential for improvement in any situation. They quite naturally notice what is right or wrong in all areas of life and are highly motivated to *improve* it. Often they intuit the best way to do a job or solve a problem very quickly. Ones are responsible, dependable people who pride themselves on their honesty and integrity. These idealists of the Enneagram can contribute ideas and energy for reform.

Dark Side of the Gift

A Perfectionist's attention to error can lead to criticism and judgment of self and others. They may believe they possess superior knowledge of the one right way. It may be difficult to recognize when something is good enough. Perfectionists exhibit a tendency to engage in black-and-white thinking. Relationships, tasks, even life are judged either good or bad, right or wrong, fair or unfair.

They often take on too much responsibility and feel resentful others don't do their share or come through with their commitments. Forsaking pleasure in favor of what *should* be done adds fuel to the fire of resentment that burns inside. Fear of making mistakes or appearing foolish can lead to procrastination in decision making.

Internal Terrain

Ones have an enormous internal critic berating and judging them, continually finding them wanting. "How could you have said something so dumb? You did that all wrong! You blew it. What were you thinking? That could have been so much better. You jerk, you idiot, you poor excuse for a human being." All of us have an inner critic, but the perfectionist's internal voice is relentless. Ones are often surprised when others accuse them of being critical, since they share only the tiniest fraction of their ongoing internal critique.

Ones are driven to do what is correct according to their own internal high standards. (Most of us would consider it nearly impossible to live up to these standards.) When Perfectionists pick up the slack or feel they must do more than their share, they become resentful of other people. It's not fair. Worse, resentment is fed by the One's own compulsion to do what *should* be done rather than what he or she wishes to do. No play or pleasure is allowed until the work and responsibilities are completed. And Perfectionists can always find more work to be done or responsibilities that need tending.

Nothing is ever perfect, so the One continues striving for improvement. Even scheduled leisure time is often spent in exercise or reading that is geared to betterment. Resentment continues to build. Most Ones do not consider themselves angry people, though the rest of us may describe them as very angry. "I don't get angry, just irritated or frustrated," Perfectionists tell us through clenched jaws. Good boys and girls don't get angry, so irritation is all that is permitted. The inner critic won't allow the genuine expression of the anger Ones stuff deep inside and it continues to simmer.

In the movie *Broadcast News*, Holly Hunter gives us a glimpse of the One's internal terrain when she confronts her boss for making what she believes to be the wrong decision. She explains her reasoning and he rejoins with, "That's your opinion."

"It's not opinion," she insists.

"You're just absolutely right. And I'm just absolutely wrong," he says in disbelief. She nods. "It must be wonderful to believe that you're the smartest person in the room. To always believe that you know best," he snarls.

"No, " she breathes, tears filling her eyes. "It's awful."

Hallmark

All characteristics do not have the same weight or importance when describing Enneagram type. In the case of the Perfectionist One, the hallmark or defining characteristic is the relentlessness of the inner critic. Many Ones describe it as a "critical voice" that constantly evaluates, judges, and harangues the Perfectionist. Some Ones are critical of other people, other Ones keep their critical thoughts to themselves. Regardless, every Perfectionist suffers from an ongoing, internal critique through nearly every minute of every day.

After reading through the characteristics of each type, Jack was confused. Was he an Eight or a One? After all, Eight fit most, but he felt that he had a pretty strong inner critic as well. He attended an Enneagram class to help him illuminate his type. After hearing the Ones describe their inner critics, he asked them, "Do you mean that you experience this critical voice almost *all* the time?" A unanimous "Yes" convinced Jack he was not a One; he only heard the critic occasionally.

A Perfectionist's Story

Dennis, an interpretive ranger in the National Park Service, tells us,

> "I didn't believe I could be a Perfectionist on the Enneagram, though I related to One more than any other type. I have a huge inner critic. Yet it always seemed to me that Ones were organized, compulsively neat people. I am anything but orderly!

> "I was lucky enough to meet a few other imperfect Perfectionists who were generally messy and disorganized. What I discovered was that I have very firm beliefs and convictions about right and wrong: in the Park Service, in employee relations and compensation, in fairness. I have very high ethical standards and work tirelessly to reform practices in my management position. I'm actually very proud of that. It's much more important to me than a neatly organized desk. I relate more to the Idealist and Reformer names for One than the Perfectionist."

(See Appendix II for various names for the nine Enneagram types.)

Type Two—the Giver

Worldview
(My) Love makes the world go round.

Beliefs
I am indispensable to my loved ones and employer, client, etc. I sense what people need and give it to them. I can help others achieve their highest potential. I don't really have any needs.

Unconscious Drive
Pride

Focus of Attention
Approval for self as helper, giver

Characteristics

- Gaining approval and avoiding rejection
- Pride in importance of oneself in relationships: "They'd never make it without me"—being indispensable
- Pride in knowing and meeting others' needs
- Giving to get—the hook
- Confusion in identifying personal needs
- Altering self to please others
- Making a difference to others' lives, the world, etc.
- Hysteria or anger when emerging real needs collide with the needs of the those one serves

Gift

Empathy—Twos have a natural ability to make empathic connections with people. Givers actually feel what others feel or need. They are driven to connect with them emotionally and fill their needs. Givers are talented networkers, making connections between and for other people. Twos may facilitate others in reaching their potential. They enjoy being the power behind the throne and enthusiastically supporting others. At their best, they are warm and caring. Twos can be true altruists, where giving is as natural as breathing and free of expectation.

Dark Side of the Gift

Twos often are so tuned into others' needs and feelings that they are not aware of their own. As a result, they can find themselves drained, and then angry. Unconscious giving has a hook in it. Givers give to get their own needs met. Givers may use warmth and flattery to get own their way. This can feel manipulative to the recipient of Twos' helpfulness. At times, Twos may give unsolicited and unwanted "help." Pride exhibits itself in the Two as a feeling of knowing what others really need.

Internal Terrain

Twos literally feel like they leave their body through their heart to empathize with others and intuit their needs. Because their attention is so directed to others, they are unaware of their own needs or feelings. But if we look at life from the perspective of the Giver, we find a conviction that survival and getting love depend on sensing and meeting the needs of others. An unacknowledged contract exists: If a Two is out there sensing and meeting our needs, we will naturally reciprocate by sensing and meeting theirs.

Those of us who live in the other eight lands of the Enneagram fail to come through with our part of the covert bargain. The Two gives until he or she is drained and comes back home to the self, exhausted. And angry! We let them down. We didn't sense their needs and we didn't give back. Self-worth depends on our gratitude and approval for their role in our lives. The connection with others is lifeblood to the Two and is guaranteed if they become necessary to us.

Hallmark

The defining characteristic for the Giver Two is the need to become central, even indispensable to another chosen individual. One Two went so far as to explain, "It's almost as if I establish my center in the person I am interested in being important to." Whether in work, friendship, or intimate relationships, the Giver believes that those significant to him or her would never make it without the Giver's help or support. The unconscious drive of pride underlies the Two's sense that they alone know what the significant other needs, and they will provide it.

A Giver's Story

Kelly, a Giver Two and a talented musician, describes becoming indispensable to her music teacher.

"I met a young friend of my parents who was a music teacher. She was bright and charming and I wanted to be just like her. I developed an interest in learning to play an instrument and found out her favorite instrument was the violin. So, wanting to be her friend and best student, I took up the violin. I figured out where she might need help, and set about making myself indispensable to her. I helped her with scheduling, recitals, and even some lessons and I didn't think she could get along without me.

"When I went away to college, however, she got along just fine. I was devastated. Along the way, I realized that I didn't really like the violin! I had never considered what *I* might like to play. I simply adopted her preference as mine, as a way of becoming closer to her. Eventually, I switched to the cello—an instrument that I like."

Type Three–the Performer

Worldview
Life is about presenting a successful image.

Beliefs
I am my accomplishments. I am the image I present. I can change my image to fit the circumstances. Everybody wants to be known as a winner.

Unconscious Drive
Self-deceit

Focus of Attention
Approval for productivity or image

Characteristics
- Goal is everything
- Efficiency
- Competition and avoidance of failure
- Love comes from what you do rather than who you are
- Feelings suspended until job gets done
- Presentation of image that's adjusted to gain approval
- Multitasking—doing several things at once
- Run over others to get to goal, apologize later

Gift
Efficacy and Adaptability—As multitasking, high-energy people, Performers get things done. They make things happen. Threes can adapt to any situation or group with a chameleon-like ability to match the environment. Performers inspire and motivate through charm and presentation of a successful image. No type on the Enneagram is more aware of the power of image. They are natural salespeople.

Dark Side of the Gift

Three's focused attention on goals and tasks can overshadow other aspects of their lives. Feelings are often relegated to the back burner in service of "doing." Performers may use others to get the task done or run over anyone who is in the way of completion. Threes may cut corners to complete goals or projects, so long as it looks good to others.

Internal Terrain

Threes can become so identified with the image they present or the things they accomplish that they lose themselves. They may not be sure of their real feelings or desires. "I'm successful at this, but do I really want to do it?" Their talent for adapting presentation to fit the audience and their identification with "doing" can leave them wondering if they have an authentic self. Dropping the image or stopping the doing will show what they've feared all along: there is nothing inside. "I am only my image." "I am only what I produce." Performers describe an overwhelming sense of being a fraud. Even legitimate accomplishments don't count. Like the Wizard of Oz, they keep maneuvering the image, hoping we won't find out they fooled us.

Like most Threes, the Wizard internally discounted his legitimate accomplishment: creating the Emerald City. As he became a redeemed or self-aware Three, he inspired those who came to him by truthfully selling them their own courage, brains, and heart. In the end, he tapped into his natural efficacy to get the balloon ready for flight back to the Midwest.

Hallmark

The defining characteristic of a Performer is excessive identification with his image or that which he produces: "I am my image" or "I am what I do." The feeling that underneath the image or productivity is a black hole of nothing is the hallmark of a Three. The Three believes that he has sold us a package of goods: himself. Fearing that he is nothing but a fraud, the Performer must keep doing, producing, selling, dazzling to keep from being found out.

A Performer's Story

Jared, a Performer Three, is a very successful fine artist. He shares,

"There are a huge number of artists out there who are much better painters than I am. But there aren't many who are as good at marketing. I know how to keep myself in the public eye, how to create a mystique about myself so that they are convinced they have to have one (or more) of my paintings. I'm constantly aware of how I can work a situation to my advantage. Even a casual encounter is an opportunity for promotion. I'm not necessarily proud of this; but it comes so naturally, I'm almost unaware of it."

Type Four—the Romantic

Worldview
Something essential is missing from life; I'll be complete if I can just find it.

Beliefs
I'm "different" from other people. No one can truly understand me or the depth of my longing. Authenticity is found in deep emotional connection. Other people have what I am missing.

Unconscious Drive
Envy

Focus of Attention
What I desire is distant; what's here and now is not what I really want.

Characteristics
- Idealization of the distant, dissatisfaction with present reality
- Sense of something missing from life—others have it
- Attachment to melancholy; deep feelings are more important than mere happiness
- Search for authenticity
- Affinity with intense in life: birth, death, etc.
- Sense of being different from others, unique, special
- Desire for emotional intensity—wants to be met emotionally
- Attraction to beauty, strong aesthetic sense
- Drawing self-esteem from externals such as mood, manners, luxury, and good taste

Gift

Uniqueness or emotional intensity—Fours have a singular ability to be present with life's more intense situations: grief, death, depression. Through their understanding of dark nights of the soul, they accompany others on their journey. Romantics model that you will eventually get through the difficult times and illuminate the riches to be found in the depths. Fours also bring originality and creativity to any enterprise. Often blessed with a strong sense of the dramatic and/or aesthetic, they are driven to make a unique contribution in life.

Dark Side of the Gift

Romantics crave emotional intensity and connection; but their highs and lows can be perceived as "too much" for the other types. A tendency toward dramatic presentation and effect can alienate other people, earning them the label of "drama queen (or king)." The Four's attraction to melancholy and the darker emotions can seem like wallowing to the rest of us. At its worst, melancholy can slide into depression. An insistence on exhibiting their uniqueness or difference can be counterproductive to their own goals and offputting to others.

Internal Terrain

Romantics feel something is missing in their life. Other people have it, but they don't. When a couple holds hands in the grocery store or a child hugs his mother, "I want what they have," the Four laments. These people seem complete and fulfilled and the Romantic envies them.

Fours believe they are different from other people. Deep inside, they feel defective, as if something essential were lacking. Longing desperately to be whole again, they search for the missing element that will complete them. "If only I could find that perfect love, job, whatever, I would be complete." But as the object of the Romantic's desire comes closer, they see its flaws and realize it doesn't make them feel whole after all. So they push it away. Then as it moves away from them, it begins to be desirable again. "Maybe that was it after all," Fours tell themselves. A push-pull pattern can develop as they continue to search for the missing piece. They are destined to be disappointed.

Fours tell us there is a bittersweet flavor to their longing and melancholy. They yearn for a deep connection where they will be met emotionally. Authenticity is found in intense emotional states, so they return there again and again. Romantics abhor anything ordinary and would rather embrace being different than be just like all the rest. And they would rather be disappointed than settle for less.

Hallmark

The hallmark or defining characteristic for the Romantic is the pervasive sense of something vital missing from his or her life. The Four doesn't know what is missing, just that it is essential to their completeness. At different times, the Romantic may decide that the missing piece is a job or a person, even a place. They will fixate on this desired object, often until it becomes attainable, then discard it or feel dissatisfied when the feeling of something missing still remains.

A Romantic's Story

Sarah, a Romantic Four, manages a busy real estate office.

"I think most people who work with me would type me as a Performer Three. That is the face I put on for work. But inside I have always been longing. My father died when I was five. I still miss him and grieve for him. Ever since my childhood, I've felt that something important was missing. And deep inside I thought that maybe it was something missing in me or at least wrong with me. I have a wonderful husband whom I love, but always secretly felt that something was missing in my relationship. The Enneagram has been a great relief to me. Finding out that I am a Four means that I can just be okay with the feeling that something is missing—and that maybe *nothing is!* It's helped me look at my marriage in a new way and feel more comfortable with my life generally."

Type Five–the Observer

Worldview

Knowledge will keep me safe.

Beliefs

People can be intrusive. People (and things) can take your private time and deplete your energy. Emotions are unpredictable and scary. Knowledge is power: It can keep you safe or be used against you.

Unconscious Drive

Avarice (greed for knowledge and privacy)

Focus of Attention
Conserving energy and gaining knowledge

Characteristics
- Privacy
- Maintaining noninvolvement, withdrawing, restraining one's emotions as the first line of defense
- Delayed emotions: feelings withheld until safely alone
- Compartmentalizing of time commitments in life
- Wanting predictability—to know what will happen
- Overvaluing self-control—drama is for lesser beings
- Interest in special knowledge and systems
- Mental clarity, detachment from emotional bias

Gift
Detachment—Observers have a natural ability to detach from feelings, needs, and other people. Clarity and a cool head prevail for the Five in situations where others become emotional and succumb to chaos. The Observer stance lends itself to keen observational powers. Fives are often good listeners; they do not push what they know onto others. Fives are independent, self-contained people. They delve deeply into areas of knowledge that excite them, often becoming experts in subjects they explore. They exhibit a highly developed capacity for systematization of thought, for analyzing and synthesizing complex information.

Dark Side of the Gift
Five's approach can be overly mental when a more feeling approach is called for. They can seem to be distant or emotionally unavailable to the other types. Observers can seem disengaged from life, preferring the mental realms of thought to interaction. Their strong need for privacy can extend toward isolation. A belief that energy is limited can lead to a compartmentalization of life. There are compartments for work, relationships, and leisure—each with its concomitant time limits. Fives can withhold information, time, energy, and even themselves.

Internal Terrain

Fives have strong feelings just like everyone else, but prefer to deal with them when they are alone and can try to understand them. It doesn't feel safe to deal with emotions in front of others; it feels out of control to the Observer. Fives tell us they only have so much energy and they need to protect their private time. Observers relate feeling overwhelmed and drained if they don't have enough alone time. Too much input is exhausting; Fives need to retreat to figure things out and understand them.

The Observer likes to know what is expected of him—then he can deliver it quickly and well. In order to discuss an emotionally charged topic, a Five needs to know when the discussion will end. They have a strong dislike of open-ended, unpredictable situations. Observers enjoy observing. They don't feel they need to join in all the time. Rather, they have a great time watching everyone else. Knowledge is very important to Observers and they prefer to keep some things to themselves. They strongly believe: "He who holds the knowledge has the power."

Hallmark

The hallmark or defining characteristic of the Observer Five is detachment. Their act of disengaging may be prompted by a social event, a family discussion, a presentation or performance, or any other interaction. Many Fives actually describe a separate "Observer self" located above or just behind them that watches them interact or perform. This keeps the Five from being overwhelmed by people, emotions, or other stimuli.

An Observer's Story

Phillip, an Observer Five, is CEO of a software company. He tells us about his fear of being overwhelmed and the need for detachment.

"It feels to me like I'm too permeable to input and energy outside me. I'm like an earthworm left on the sidewalk in the rain. He can't keep out the water and if he doesn't get out of the rain, he'll absorb so much he'll explode. I've learned to just 'go away' in situations where I feel overwhelmed, even though my body is technically still there. It really is like I watch myself from a distance, talking, being witty, doing what needs to be done until I can get away by myself for a while and recharge."

Type Six—the Loyal Skeptic

Worldview

The world is a dangerous place; most people have hidden agendas.

Beliefs

If you relax your vigilance, you become prey. Authority is not to be trusted. People say one thing and mean another. If you plan for the worst-case scenario, you can keep yourself safe.

Unconscious Drive

Fear—doubt

Centering prayer is good. Julian prayer

Focus of Attention

Worst-case scenarios and hidden motives — *fear of abandonment*

Characteristics

- Scan environment for clues that explain inner sense of threat
- Intuitive style of powerful imagination and single-pointed attention, both natural to the fearful mind
- Authority problems—distrust
- Identification with underdog causes
- Issues with incompletion—success is exposure to danger
- Suspicious of others' motives: bullshit detecting
- Skepticism and doubt
- Analysis paralysis: thinking replaces doing
- Heightened fear when things are going well—when's the other shoe going to drop?

Gift

Loyal commitment and planning—Sixes' strong powers of imagination enable them to see the pitfalls, downside, or dangers of any situation. Masterful planners, Loyal Skeptics visualize ways to deal with or avoid these dangers. Sixes exhibit tremendous loyalty to a cause or person they believe in. They are often committed, dutiful, behind-the-scenes workers or team players.

Dark Side of the Gift

Sixes' highly developed sense of danger can be activated even when the potential threat is actually very low. The other types may feel Loyal Skeptics are messengers of doom and gloom or excessive worriers. Like the boy who cried wolf, they can lose credibility with constant alarmist messages and be discounted when a true danger or pitfall is imminent. Loyalty of the Six can be misplaced and go against their own best interest. Commitment and duty can exhaust and overwhelm the Six.

Two Flavors of Six: Flight Six and Fight Six

The Loyal Skeptic Six has two very different manifestations that correspond to the human reaction to situations that evoke fear: fight or flight. In Enneagram lingo, we call the Flight Six "Phobic" and the Fight Six "Counterphobic" (literally, against phobic).

Phobic or Flight Sixes are aware they are fearful and vigilantly scan the environment for that which is threatening. They make plans for preventing or escaping the worst case. Avoiding confrontation with authority, they use charm to disarm those they feel might be threatening.

On the other hand, Fight Six Counterphobics are aware they are driven by fear. Indeed, they may think of themselves as fearless. Consequently, they cultivate daredevil pursuits such as motorcycle racing or parachute jumping. The Fight Six can visualize the worst-case scenario just as well as the Flight Six can, but prefers not to dwell on it. Quickly they jump into action with both feet, effectively overcoming and overriding their fear. Yet they may inadvertently get themselves into dangerous situations through this reaction against fear. Counterphobic Sixes will confront authority or those they mistrust to provoke them into showing their true colors.

Both Phobic and Counterphobic Sixes have ambivalent feelings about those in authority. Because they believe most people have hidden motives, they are doubtful, skeptical, and drawn to underdog causes. Both flavors of Six may suffer from overthinking situations, difficulties with success, waiting for the other shoe to drop when things are going well, and the ability to see the pitfalls or downsides of any situation. Both share the gifts of loyalty and planning.

Internal Terrain

"Some call me a pessimist, but in truth I am a realist," proclaims the Loyal Skeptic. Sixes see the dangers that exist all around us and believe it makes no sense to be caught unprepared. They can instantly visualize the downside or danger in any situation and may actually see it in the mind's eye—as if it were happening in real time. Sixes experience the fear reaction in their bodies as if the imagined event were actually taking place. After imagining the worst case, Loyal Skeptics make a plan to deal with the pitfalls or dangers. They stay vigilant at all times.

When a real danger presents itself, a Six moves into action and fear drops away. "Fear lives in my imagination. But when the worst actually happens, I can be clear and effective. I'm ready for it; after all, I knew it would happen," a Six informs us. Loyal Skeptics keep looking for an authority that can be trusted, but believe that most people in authority abuse their power. If Sixes find a cause they believe in, they will fight to the death for it. After all, they've already imagined death as the ultimate worst-case scenario. If they choose to make a commitment, they will go to the mat. Sixes generally prefer to work behind the scenes rather than to have positions of power or authority. To them, success signals danger and serving as the point person only exposes them as targets.

Hallmark

The hallmark of the Loyal Skeptic involves seeing the downside or danger almost immediately, whether it involves visualizing a worst-case scenario in graphic detail or ferreting out hidden motives. The Phobic or Flight Six reacts with fear and avoidance of danger while the Counterphobic or Fight Six jumps in with both feet to prove they can overcome potential pitfalls. Yet both will imagine the worst case. In the matter of hidden motives, the Phobic Six may be watchful and wary while the Counterphobic Six will confront, poking and prodding to unmask ulterior motives. In reality, most Sixes are not purely Phobic or Counterphobic; but a combination of both.

A Loyal Skeptic's Story

Caldwell, a retired advertising executive, describes himself as a Counterphobic Six with an immediate focus on hidden motives.

"While I was visiting my daughter and her husband, I noticed a picture of a child on the refrigerator and asked who she
was. My daughter told me she was a Guatemalan child they
had 'adopted' by sending money to a relief agency once a month.
Before I could stop myself, I voiced my first thought, 'I'll bet
there are a hundred pictures of the same kid on a hundred other
refrigerators.' My daughter was horrified. But my first thought
really was: This is a scam perpetrated by someone with a hidden motive to steal money from guilt-ridden childless couples."

Type Seven—The Optimist

Worldview
Life is an adventure with limitless possibilities.

Beliefs
Life is about experiencing as much as possible. There are too many
wonderful options to spend time wallowing in pain and difficulty. Closing down options is like being trapped. Even bad things are good because
you learn something from them.

Unconscious Drive
Gluttony (for life experience)

Focus of Attention
Pleasant future options, fun

Characteristics
- Sustaining high levels of excitement; many activities, many inter-
  esting things to do
- Endless possibilities—can lead to dilettantism
- Feel trapped without multiple options or a way out
- Life is about fun and adventure—sampling all of it
- Avoidance of pain or difficulty
- Reframing any negative into a positive
- Replacement of deep contact with pleasant mental alternatives:
  talking, planning, intellectualizing
- Charm as first line of defense—fear type who moves toward people

- Equalizing authority
- Making unusual connections between unrelated ideas

Gift

Optimism—The optimistic Seven sees the bright side of any situation. A high energy, upbeat person, the Optimist can sweep others up in his or her enthusiasm. They enjoy envisioning possibilities and options. Sevens are great "idea" people spinning out seemingly endless visions and potentials. Planning for future pleasure and fun is a major preoccupation of the Optimist. Sevens are synergistic thinkers who make connections between seemingly unlike things.

Dark Side of the Gift

The Seven's one-sided focus on the bright side of life can lead them to neglect an entire realm of human experience. Sadness, pain, loss, and difficulty are assiduously avoided by the Optimist. Others may find that the Seven cannot be counted on to be there in times of crisis, or even to address serious issues. The archetypal child who never grows up, the Seven rushes greedily to the next experience or sensation. In the movie *Auntie Mame* the title character expressed the Seven life view when she proclaimed "Life is a banquet—and most poor suckers are starving to death." Their ability to reframe problems into positives may lead Optimists to dismiss the real downsides of life.

Sevens feel trapped by any limitation on options. This can lead to difficulties with commitment—to tasks, people, or both. Optimists spin out ideas and visions prodigiously but may not complete projects. Sevens can be dilettantes trying a variety of jobs, hobbies, sports, yet moving on to something new before becoming truly proficient at any single enterprise.

Internal Terrain

To Sevens, life is just too wonderful to waste time wallowing in pain or sadness. They can't understand why other people do. Why be down when you can be up? Most Optimists relate that from childhood, they've had the ability to see something good in even the worst situations. Life's possibilities are endless to Sevens and they want to sample as much of life's offerings as they can.

Sevens get bored easily and like to try new experiences. They don't like to be limited and prefer to have plenty of options open, even if they don't avail themselves of them. When a Seven has had a great idea or vision, they almost feel like they've done it already—in their mind. So it isn't necessarily important to them to finish a project they've started. They've already had the satisfaction of the idea. When bored, the Seven just moves on to something new. Deep down inside, Optimists are afraid of the pain of feeling trapped by limits on their options. A Seven's greatest fear is that if they were to actually feel their pain and sadness, it would consume or annihilate them.

Hallmark

The hallmark or defining characteristic of an Optimist Seven is that of reframing any negative into a positive. Sevens see the good in everything, often to their own detriment. They focus on the silver lining and miss the fact that the dark cloud exists. Even trauma and tragedy are reframed into good learning experiences or humorous stories: "Yes, my dad beat me, but what was good about it was . . . ."

An Optimist's Story

Carlotta, an Optimist Seven, shares a seminal moment when her reframing went too far—even for her.

want to run from anything unpleasant

"My husband and I had lost our youngest child at the age of three months to SIDS [Sudden Infant Death Syndrome or crib death]. Five months later, I was at a party telling a close friend that everything was all right now, that my husband and I were pretty much through it when I saw a look of horror on her face. I suddenly realized I had been smiling, telling her how positive it was that my baby had died and given my husband and me this opportunity for growing closer. In that moment, I saw myself as she saw me—and I was horrified. There is nothing good about losing your child, nothing at all. I was overwhelmed with grief and went into therapy shortly thereafter."

Type Eight–The Straight Shooter

Worldview

Only the strong survive.

Beliefs

The truth comes out in a good fight. The world is black and white: strong or weak, friend or foe. Life is to be lived passionately, lustily, with nothing held back. Too much of a good thing is almost enough. Weak is unworthy. I protect my own.

Unconscious Drive
Lust (excess)

Focus of Attention
Control

Characteristics
- Control of personal space, possessions, and people likely to influence Eight's life
- Aggression and open expression of anger
- Action before thinking, impulsiveness
- Concern with justice and protection of others
- Sparring as a way of making contact—trusting those who can hold their own in a fight
- Excess as antidote to boredom: too much exercise, work, partying, etc.
- Difficulty in recognizing dependent aspects of self
- All-or-nothing way of seeing world: weak or strong, fair or unfair, etc.
- Impatience with indecision and inaction

Gift
Strength—Eights are straightforward, direct, what-you-see-is-what-you-get people. They are able to take charge and make decisions quickly. Straight Shooters are people of action. They can inspire others to do more than they thought possible by the sheer force of their will. Eights often act as protectors of the weak and promoters of justice. Straight Shooters are ebullient, larger-than-life leaders who partake of life's pleasures with all their being. As such, they are sensate people who respond to the elements: wind, water, rock, and storm.

Dark Side of the Gift
Eight's direct, no-nonsense approach can feel brutal and controlling to others. Unaware of their impact, they can steamroll over the emotions and wishes of others to get their own way. Decisions made quickly by gut instinct may not be adequately tempered with thought

or feeling. Eights can divide the world into those who are worthy and those who are not. Those who are deserving (according to the Eight) fall under the Straight Shooter's protective wing. Others deemed weak and unworthy seem almost caricature-like to the Eight and are simply "eaten" or vanquished. The laws of the jungle apply in the Straight Shooter's worldview. Lust for life can lead to excesses dangerous to health and hearth—drugs, alcohol, exercise. Others can see the Eight as too much, too loud, too everything.

Internal Terrain

"I don't care if you like me, but you'd better respect me," the Eight asserts. Straight Shooters enjoy a good fight with a worthy adversary because they believe the truth comes out in a fight. Eights like it when others stand up to them—they enjoy finding out what others are made of. Straight Shooters have a hard time holding back their emotions when angry. Yet an Eight's anger is brief and intense as a summer storm: When it's over, it's over.

A Straight Shooter can't help taking command of a situation; if there is a space, the Straight Shooter will expand to fill it. Eights don't actually feel it is important that they be the person in control; they just don't want to be controlled. Often it's easier to just take charge to avoid being controlled—a sort of preemptive strike by the Straight Shooter.

Eights despise wishy-washy people who can't make decisions. They are impatient with excess mentation or emoting. Straight Shooters tell us that when they are enjoying something, they want to do it full-force, no holds barred. As one Eight said, "If it's good, just kill me with it. Some people call that excess. I figure, why do it if you're not going to do it all the way?"

In reality, Straight Shooters assiduously avoid their own vulnerability. Since they secretly fear they might be weak deep down inside, they convert their softer feelings into boredom and find the antidote in a lust for life. Eights tend to make intimate contact through sex and fighting.

Hallmark

The hallmark or defining characteristic of Eight is bigger-than-life energy. Regardless of physical stature, Straight Shooters just seem to take up a lot of space. This larger-than-life quality manifests as abundant, even excessive energy. Eights seem able to do more, for longer periods than the rest of us.

Oddly enough, many Straight Shooters haven't a clue they take up more space than others or even that they have more energy. Yet everyone else around them is all too aware. If the characteristics and worldview sound familiar to you, but you are unsure about the hallmark, elicit the perception of family, coworkers, and friends to find out if they see you as larger-than-life.

A Straight Shooter's Story

Caitlin, a diminutive Straight Shooter Eight, is a senior flight attendant for a major airline. She shares her perception of her energy, as well as those of others.

> "I realized early on that I took up a lot of space, especially on an aircraft where actual physical space is limited. I've been told I intimidate the other flight attendants when they are too slow in making decisions.

> "Realizing I am impatient, I've been working on it. Recently I've become aware of how big my energy really can be. When I am clear with decisions or agenda, I can sometimes feel the other person shrink back or even get smaller somehow. It creates what I call a 'power void.' My usual reaction is to immediately fill the void with my presence. I don't even have to take a step, I just get 'bigger.' I'm really trying hard now just to allow the void, to stay centered in myself. I don't need to take over all the space. When I'm not self-aware, when I'm personally on autopilot, I still fill that power void automatically. It's just natural."

Type Nine—the Mediator

Worldview

Life is about harmony—going with the flow.

Beliefs

Having one's own agenda or preferences disrupts harmony, so its better to just go along with others. Nothing really matters that much anyway. Conflict is to be avoided at all costs.

Unconscious Drive
Sloth (self-forgetting: laziness toward own agenda and desires)

Focus of Attention
Other people's agendas

Characteristics
- Go with the flow—merging with others and the universe
- Self-forgetting: laziness toward own needs, priorities, agenda
- Trouble with decisions: Do I agree or disagree? Do I want to be here or not?
- Containment of physical energy and anger
- Replace essential needs with nonessential substitutes—the most important things are left until the end of the day
- Act through habit and repeating familiar solutions
- Control through stubbornness and passive-aggressive behavior
- Numbing out, inertia, running on automatic pilot

Gift
Acceptance—Nines are the great receivers of the Enneagram; open and accepting of others without judgment. An affable, calm demeanor exemplifies these easygoing people. Able to sense others' internal states, Nines are capable of merging into deep connection with others. Through this understanding comes an ability to see all sides of an issue and to play peacemaker between warring factions. Mediators value being (as opposed to doing) and often live in the present moment.

Dark Side of the Gift
Indiscriminate merging with the agendas and priorities of others to avoid disharmony leaves the Nine asleep to his or her own preferences. The Mediator can adopt a passive role and wait for others to determine the course. Living in the present moment can make planning and prioritizing for the future a difficult task. Seeing all things as equal can then interfere with decision making and lead to procrastination. The Nine's desire for peace can curtail healthy conflict and problem solving. The laws of inertia may be said to apply to Mediators—when in action they can keep going indefinitely, but when they stop it may take

a lot of energy to get them going again. Peaceful affect of Nines can be interpreted as low energy or sluggishness by others.

Internal Terrain

Nines generally find it easier to go along with others' preferences rather than to try to find their own. First, it's difficult for Mediators to know what they want. Second, they don't want to risk their desire conflicting with that of someone important to them. Nines like life to be peaceful and comfortable. Because all viewpoints and input seem equal to Nines, it's easy for them to act as a mediator. However, "all things being equal" causes a great deal of turmoil inside the individual Nine. Everything needing to be done or attended to clamors for their attention, and they are unable to prioritize or act. Sometimes, they numb themselves with TV, books, or food to help stop the inner chaos.

When Nines "space out" or narcotize themselves, it can be difficult for them to get started again. The laws of inertia apply to the Mediator. A body in motion tends to remain in motion, while a body at rest tends to remain at rest. Nines relate that they often get energized by being around other people; it's much harder to get energized on their own. Mediators' ability to merge with others' viewpoints makes it easy for them to accept people just as they are. Nines don't see why everyone can't just get along.

Hallmark

The Mediator Nine often overlooks or "forgets" his own agenda, desires, and priorities, which seem to be hidden or unclear. The underlying drive of sloth leads the Nine to go with the flow rather than work to determine what they really want or need. Instead, Nines find it easier to adopt or merge with the preferences and desires of other people.

Although this can seem similar to the stance of the Giver Two, it differs in that Mediator Nines merge indiscriminately with others. It just "happens." Giver Twos are very selective in choosing the people whose priorities they make their own. The Two stance very actively moves toward others, while the Nines are more passive, allowing them to go along with others. As with all the characteristics for all nine types, self-forgetting can get to be a habit.

A Mediator's Story

Daphne, a Mediator Nine, developed with another woman a painting methodology to unlock the creativity of the ordinary person. After fifteen years, they split the business and went their separate ways. Five years after the split, Daphne recalls an illuminating moment of self-forgetting.

> "I was giving an introductory lecture to a large group of business people who had hired me as a creativity coach. I explained the method in detail and showed a number of slides to illustrate. At the end of the first session, someone in the audience raised his hand and asked why all the slides in the show were either those of my former business partner or of students. I was shocked to realize I had never put a single slide of my own work in the show! I simply 'forgot' myself and my own contributions."

Narrowing the Search for Type

Perhaps you recognized yourself in more than one of the Enneagram types described above. That is to be expected early in the process of discovering your type. It's best if we look at our personality or type as our default mode. On most computer programs, a predetermined group of options or preferences is set for us (such as font, size of type, etc.). This pre-set mode is called the default mode. When we become more comfortable working the program, we begin to override the default mode and choose our own preferences. Then we have more flexibility and can tailor the program to fit our needs in a particular document or situation.

In much the same way, our Enneagram type is merely our default mode. Our personality is a preset way of being. But we are not limited to this one way of being, perceiving, and acting. Indeed, the majority of us by midlife will have availed ourselves of many of the modes of being described by the Enneagram in different situations or at different times in our life. However, whenever we go on automatic or are unconscious of our behavior, we revert back to our default mode.

One way to find our type is to notice when we fall into our default mode. Chances are we won't notice when we are in that mode—but we will become aware just after we have left it. Being on autopilot, letting the personality run the show without being aware of it is like driving somewhere without noticing how you got there. Suddenly you realize you don't remember driving to the location. Yet you must have—you arrived in your car! It's as if you were on automatic, unaware, and then suddenly you came back to yourself and are aware again. That moment of awareness can occur when you realize you were enacting a pattern that is so familiar, you don't realize you are doing it until after the fact. That lets you see the pattern that is your personality in its default mode.

Another help to discovering our Enneagram type is to look back at how we acted, felt, and perceived the world when in our late teens or early twenties. Enneagram theory relates that we are probably most purely "on point" or in our default mode as young adults. As we grow, we learn more ways of coping, behaving, and seeing in the world beyond the home base of our Enneagram type.

Thirdly, we often identify not only with our core type, but also with those points or types we access under conditions of stress or comfort and security. We may find that we identify two or three types as strong within us—only to discover they are our stress point or security point. They may also be wing points. Movement under stress and security, as well as wings, will be examined in more depth in Chapter 4.

The next chapter on energy and centers of intelligence of the Enneagram types will illuminate further aspects of personality and may help you narrow your search for your own type and the types of others in your life. Energy, as you will see, is a critical component for understanding and meeting others in ways that foster honoring and connection. Knowing your own energetic can help you learn to keep from overwhelming or underwhelming others and to relate in productive ways.

 # Energy, Centers of Intelligence, and the Enneagram

Determining your point on the Enneagram of personality is best accomplished as a personal journey of self-discovery. The journey may be short or long depending on a number of factors: how well you know your internal terrain, how much you've camouflaged your natural personality to get along in the world, and the amount of time and attention you spend noticing your thoughts, feelings, and actions.

A number of written tests have been developed that purport to find your Enneagram type. Unfortunately, results have been inconclusive (ambiguous) at best and just plain wrong at worst. Nevertheless, a written test can be useful in beginning the process of inquiry into your habitual way of thinking, feeling, and acting.

Why don't the tests conclusively ascertain our type? The Enneagram describes a worldview, certain beliefs and traits associated with that worldview, and habitual ways of perceiving and being in everyday life. Many of these aspects of type can be elucidated through pencil and paper tests. However, a very important element eludes reduction to multiple choice questions: the "energy" of each of the Enneagram types. That's right—energy.

Energy is the manifestation of the life force in each of us. We "sense" the energy or substance of another individual whenever we come in contact with him. We feel if he "takes up a lot of space" or seems "lightweight," if he seems "down to earth" or "transparent, almost invisible." These descriptions by ordinary people about others embody what we mean by energy. We don't physically see this energy, yet we have a sense of the substance or life force of another even if we don't think of it as energy. Each of the types has a specific energetic, a type of energy based on the primary *center of intelligence* utilized by the type. Each type also expresses a basic underlying emotion. How that basic, subconscious emotion is addressed by each particular type contributes to the energetic.

Centers of Intelligence—Making Sense of Our World

We perceive and interpret information from the environment through our five senses of hearing, seeing, taste, touch, and smell. Each of these senses has its own intelligence, adding to our conception and experience of the world around us. Yet we have more than these five senses to help us make sense of our environment and the people in it. We also take in vital information through three additional senses or *centers of intelligence*, which—though less well-known—are indispensable to understanding how we develop a worldview. These centers are the head or visionary center, the heart or emotional center, and the gut or instinctual center. All humans have all three centers of intelligence, although we may not access each of them equally.

Accordingly, the nine types of the Enneagram can be grouped into three "triads" (or groups of three) based on the primary center of intelligence through which the various types understand the world and formulate their reactions. These centers are like complementary *organs of perception* that help us make sense of our environment and relationships. Types Five, Six, and Seven share the head as the primary center or *organ of perception*. The heart is the primary center for types Two, Three, and Four. And types Eight, Nine, and One use primarily the gut center.

Head Center—Visionary

The head center is useful in logical reasoning, abstract thought, the use of language and symbols, and imagery. It is also the organ of perception involved in planning, memory, strategizing, and envisioning pitfalls and possibilities. Our dreams and our visions of the future are created in the head center. We synthesize information and make mental connections here. It is the center that we most commonly associate with understanding and intelligence.

When many of us first attended school, we discovered we were to use the head center as our primary intelligence for learning. IQ tests were based on head center skills such as memory and logical or abstract thought. Fives, Sixes, and Sevens probably felt right at home. Unfortunately, six out of nine the Enneagram types were asked to value the head center over their primary learning and understanding center. Small wonder that many of us felt misunderstood or had difficulty adapting to "head centered" learning.

Heart Center—Emotional

The heart center is important to our emotional life. This is the center where we feel connection to other beings as well as to ourselves. It is the repository of our love, empathy, and compassion. Love and loss, bliss and pain reside in the heart. Our ability to intuit how we appear to others is located in this center of intelligence. Through the heart center, we tap into others' approval or disapproval of us and feel what adjustments will shift their perceptions. Although Fours often make adjustments *against* what will gain another's approval—to prove their uniqueness and that no one can understand them—make no mistake, they are just as concerned with how they are perceived as are Twos and Threes.

Gut Center—Instinctual

The gut center is the instinctual and sensate center in the belly, below the umbilicus, through which the world is sensed or felt. It senses not only the spatial location of objects and people in the environment, but also the elemental, the realms of wind, rain, earth, rock, and storm. This is the center of our intuition or "gut knowing" that instinctively knows the "best" way to do something. The gut senses conflict vs. harmony in the environment even when no words are spoken. This is the center of our power, our strength, and our instinctual knowing

The Centers of Intelligence in Daily Life

Let's look at the contribution of these three centers of intelligence to an everyday decision faced by each of us at some point in life—finding a home or place to live.

We look at the factual information: how far we'll need to travel to work, whether it fits our price range, if it is close to shopping or schools, or other services. We look at the rooms, imagine how we might decorate them, and what we might change to fit our vision of a home. All of these are the purview of the head center.

The intelligence of the heart center is concerned with connection—is this a place where we might feel connected to ourselves and others? How will our friends and family feel about this move? Will we make new friends or feel connected to our neighbors? Do we feel emotionally drawn here? Do we anticipate living in this new space, even though we feel a sense of loss for our old home?

The gut center helps us sense the layout of the space—the feel of the rooms, whether expansive or cozy, open or protected. We get an idea of the area, the neighborhood from our gut. Is it friendly or adversarial, safe or hostile, open or secluded? Our gut instinct tells us if this is the right neighborhood, house, or place for us.

All of the intelligence of the three centers comes into play when we are making a decision. If all three are in agreement that the choice is right, the decision is easy. If there is conflict among the intelligences, we may struggle to "think it through." Or we may decide against the move, waiting until it "feels right." However, we may not be able to articulate why we chose as we did, if we are only aware of our head or mental center as the intelligence behind our decision-making process.

On the occasions we *have* been aware of using the heart and gut centers' abilities as part of our everyday life, we may have learned to discount them, to devalue their contribution, or to hide our reliance on them. As we learn the role of each of the centers' intelligences, we may avail ourselves of their perspectives. The information derived from all three of these centers is vital to our becoming fully conscious, fully functioning human beings. And because this sensing or emotional intelligence is an innate part of being human, we can re-incorporate or remember these abilities with only a little practice.

Exercise: Three Centers Decision-Making Recall

Think back to an important decision you made in your life. You can most likely recall the role the three centers of intelligence played in your decision-making process. Do you remember how thinking, feeling, and sensing contributed to the outcome? What did your head tell you? Your heart? Your gut? Were they in agreement?

Exercise: *Three Centers Decision-Making Practice*

To hone our ability to become mindful in all life's situations and to utilize the important resources at our disposal, we need to employ these three centers of intelligence—again and again. For the next decision you have to make, consciously assess its parameters with all three centers of your intelligence. How does your head inform you? What is your heart telling you? How about your gut? Are they in harmony or in conflict?

Energy and the Three Triads

Feeling and sensing the energy of people and our environment are aspects of emotional intelligence and therefore natural to us as human beings. It is the skills and talents of the heart and gut centers that combine to form our emotional and sensory intelligence. Daniel Goleman, in his excellent books on emotional intelligence, refers to these abilities as our EQ or emotional intelligence quotient.

Many of us may not have cultivated these aptitudes, due to underestimating their importance in our daily lives. Yet we use them all the time, whether we are aware of it or not. We notice the energetic of each person we meet, though we usually don't use the word energy to describe them. We might say, "She really takes up a lot of space." "I feel uplifted and excited just being around him." "It feels like she doesn't have much flexibility once a decision's been made." "It's like his body's in the room, but he's somewhere else."

Each of the Enneagram types exerts its own energetic, as though each has a "force field" that contains its own particular life force or energy. What is this energy? The dictionary uses *substance, intensity, spirit,* and *strength* as synonyms. We might call it a vibration that our emotional intelligence tunes into.

Furthermore, each triad of the Enneagram is driven by an emotion linked to the primary intelligence center. The head triad is driven by fear, the heart triad by grief, and the gut triad by anger. Individual types within the triad play out the emotion in different ways. In each group of three, one type externalizes the emotion, one type internalizes the emotion, and the third type has "forgotten" that emotion. The underlying emotion and the primary center of intelligence seem to "create" the energy or force field of each type. Therefore, the force field is embodied very differently by each of the Enneagram types.

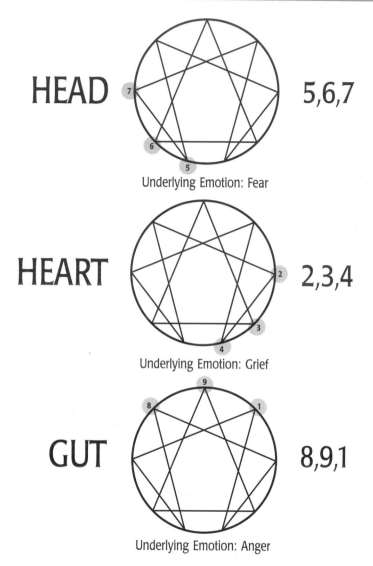

HEAD   **5,6,7**

Underlying Emotion: Fear

HEART   **2,3,4**

Underlying Emotion: Grief

GUT   **8,9,1**

Underlying Emotion: Anger

Figure 3-1 *Three centers of mental and emotional intelligence.*

In attempting to recognize another person's type, sensing his or her energy or force field can be invaluable. People may embody all the traits and characteristics of the Enneagram types at different times and in different situations. But it is the energy we feel through our emotional intelligence that gives us clues as to how they come at the world and can narrow down their type for us.

In the following descriptions of each type and the effect of its force field on the rest of us, we gain a map-reading tool in finding another individual's type on the Enneagram schematic. It may help in our understanding of the specific manifestation of the force field for each type to examine the triad, the underlying emotion, and the drive the emotion fuels. Let's take a look at the energy of the individual types.

The Head Triad—Types Five, Six, and Seven

Fear is the ruling emotion in the head center triad and types Five, Six, and Seven react in a manner peculiar to each.

Observer Five

Triad: Head
Emotion: Fear internalized
Drive: Avarice
Energy: "Invisible" detachment

Five represents the internalized version of fear. The mental center creates a haven to which Fives can retreat. There the realm of ideas and knowledge will keep one safe. The drive for the Five is avarice: greed for knowledge and privacy. Observers fear being overwhelmed by outside stimuli, emotions, or events (surprises) for which they can't prepare. Their strategic defense of withdrawal includes the retreat of their life force to an internal safe place, like a castle with the drawbridge pulled up.

Those of us who inhabit the rest of the Enneagram points experience this absence of vital being. The energy is simply "not there." The body is present and seems to occupy space, but the force field is gone. As a result, the Five can avoid being "seen" and their presence at a meeting or event may not be remembered. As we try to find the Five, energetically, we may bring about the very feeling of intrusion they dread. If the Five has not withdrawn, we can experience running into a very strong boundary when we intrude. We seem to bounce off a powerful force field—a seeming "get back" vibe.

When dealing with a Five's energy, take special care to pull your own force field back close to your body. Be careful not to overwhelm the Five with your energy. Respect the Five's strong boundaries.

Loyal Skeptic Six

Triad: Head
Emotion: Fear externalized
Drive: Fear/doubt
Energy: Flight Six—"poised for flight" scanning; Fight Six—jabbing confrontation

Six is the externalized version of fear. The mental center's capacity for imagination is highly developed in the Loyal Skeptic Six, who continually imagines the worst-case scenario, and then plans to keep himself safe. Doubt is the drive that manifests as a natural outgrowth of fear— and Sixes doubt nearly everything.

Six's two manifestations of Flight and Fight have very different ways of expressing fear, hence they have very different energetics. Phobic or Flight Six asks for confirmation. They scan the environment for dangers. Charm and warmth are used to disarm potential enemies. A childlike sweetness can evoke protector impulses in the rest of us. Their energy is high up around the head and out from the body in a full 360 degrees—swirling and scanning the environment like radar. Like a fearful rabbit, energy comes forward and scurries back in a repeating pattern as trust develops.

The Fight Six jumps right in with both feet when up against a scary, dangerous world. Action is the antidote to fear. They may even purposely engage in daredevil pursuits to exert control over or conquer their fear. Hidden motives can be brought to light if you confront others—provoke them until the truth comes out.

Not surprisingly, the energy of the Fight Six can feel jabbing to the rest of us. There is a push, then a withdrawal of the force field. Another push, withdrawal. It is the energetic equivalent of the Cowardly Lion confronting the Scarecrow and Tin Man. The Fight Six checks us out like a prizefighter circling his opponent, waiting for the worst.

Keep your answers, promises, and energy rock-solid when dealing with a Six. Stay focused and in your body. Don't react to the Fight Six by pushing your force field at him—like the Cowardly Lion when slapped by Dorothy, he'll crumple.

Optimist Seven

Triad: Head
Emotion: Fear forgotten
Drive: Gluttony
Energy: Airy excitement

Sevens are also driven by fear but have forgotten they are afraid. The mental center is used as a diversion from what invokes fear, by imagining pleasant future options and possibilities. Even memory can be affected, so that only pleasant memories are easily recalled or a positive interpretation is placed on remembered, painful events.

The drive for the Optimist Seven is Gluttony—for life experience, adventure, and possibility. So the Seven races from course to course, frenetically sampling life's banquet in an effort to stay high and optimistic.

The energy of Sevens feels airy and effervescent and their excitement can be contagious, but also exhausting. Like a ping pong ball giddily bouncing in a chaotic pattern, the Optimist is the energetic equivalent of Peter Pan, grabbing ideas like fairy dust from the air, then sprinkling and leaving them just as quickly when something else has grabbed their attention. If you try to focus or limit a Seven, swooooosh—their energy is out the door to Never-Neverland, even if their body remains in the room.

It is easy to get caught up in an Optimist's enthusiastic energy and lose focus. When dealing with a Seven, stay focused and centered. Keep your own energy or force field lower in your body, closer to the ground. This will help prevent your getting caught up in the Seven's whirlwind of visions and ideas, losing sight of your own priorities.

The Heart Triad—Types Two, Three, and Four

Two, Three, and Four make up the heart center triad. The emotion that fuels their drives is grief. Other Enneagram authors also refer to this triad as the "image" triad, due to these three types' concern with how others perceive them. Grief or sadness ensues when each feels he or she has *substituted* an image as full or partial replacement for the Self.

Giver Two

Triad: Heart
Emotion: Grief externalized
Drive: Pride
Energy: Aggressive affection

Point Two is the externalized version of grief. The Giver feels others' feelings, empathizes with their pain, and works to meet their needs and heal them. A Two has an image of himself as the Giver and caretaker, the one without needs who can intuit and meet the needs of others. The charge of the emotional battery is externalized to others by the Two, so they don't need to feel their own. Of course the downside of this occurs when the Two's battery is discharged until it is empty.

The drive for Two is pride. The Two tells a story of feeling energy coming out from the middle of the chest to another with whom they desire connection. They divine through their emotional center what the significant person needs. Unfortunately, because their life force is externalized and probing others, they are out of touch with themselves. Their pride shows itself in that they believe they know not only another's needs, but also how to meet those needs. Another aspect of pride is reflected in the Giver's belief that they have no needs of their own.

Those of us who attract the Two's focused attention feel the intensity of being the center of the Two's universe. Our intrinsic value is verified by the Two. The energy feels like a warm, aggressive force field coming from the Giver's heart toward us, enfolding us. This can feel either wonderful or intrusive.

When a Two is overwhelmed or frenetically giving, they can fall victim to a swirling chaos of emotions or hysteria. Although this energy is like an emotional tornado, it is important for us to stay present and solid when hysteria erupts. Givers already fear we will abandon them—if we stay steady, offer focused clarity, and do not leave the room, the Two will profoundly appreciate this. And we will avoid getting caught up in the maelstrom of hysteria.

Performer Three

Triad: Heart
Emotion: Grief forgotten
Drive: Deceit
Energy: Charismatic connection

Three is the member of the heart triad who simply has forgotten his or her grief. Performer Threes are busy, optimistic people. They set aside the emotional charge of their grief when channeling enormous amounts of energy into doing and presenting a successful image to others. The Three then appears very driven—a workaholic. They are prodigious producers. Grief is an emptiness Threes learn to avoid by juggling multiple tasks and projects, or adjusting their image to be seen as successful.

The Performers' habit of deceit is mainly self-deceit, in that they deceive themselves into believing they *are* the image they project. "I am what I do" or "I am my image" displaces authentic desires and preoccupations. Threes trick themselves into believing they *are* whatever will gain them success in others' eyes. On a deeper level, Performers believe there is no authentic Self underneath the image, so they'd better keep dazzling you with their successful performance. Otherwise you could see there is nothing but smoke and mirrors covering an empty hole.

Swirling like smoke and brilliant like mirrors, the Performer Three's energy is captivating. It is moving and shaking, inspiring energy. We listen with bated breath—suspending our own disbelief—when Three comes toward us from the heart, simultaneously divining and making the subtle image shifts that will gain our love. A Five described a famous Three politician: "I saw him speak and I was so uplifted and inspired, I would have followed him anywhere. Later, I tried to recall what he said and I couldn't come up with a single concrete position. And I consider myself a critical thinker."

Romantic Four

Triad: Heart
Emotion: Grief internalized
Drive: Envy
Energy: Dramatic pull

Four represents the internalized version of grief in the Heart triad. Romantic Fours tell a tale of loss and longing for a pivotal missing piece that is central to their feeling whole and complete. Rather than externalize grief like the Twos (others need help, I don't), Fours internalize and focus on their sadness. In fact, the Four may amplify or intensify the sadness in order to explore it deeply. An image that reveals the Romantic's uniqueness or defectiveness in others' eyes, serves to enhance and continue the feeling of loss that no one else can understand. The emotional charge of grief is found in the Four's rich inner life of bittersweet longing.

Envy grows out of this grief and becomes the Four's drive. Not only is the Four missing some elemental piece that would make life complete, but it is clear *others* have it. The Four longs for the completeness, the love, others have. If Romantics fixate attention on a person (or job, place, whatever) they feel will complete them, they feel the tug of their heartstrings toward the desired.

The rest of the Enneagram points feel the Four's heart as if it were pulling at them. Romantic Fours do not want to leave their rich inner world, but rather to bring the other to them, to join and make them finally complete. Energetically, there can be a magnetic pull toward the Four's depth. Even their energy seems special, somehow different. The difference pulls seductively.

As the object of the Four's desire comes closer to being realized, the Four may find flaws and push it away. So energy can pull—and then push away. As the desired person or object recedes into the distance, it may become desired again, and the Four pulls it back toward him or her. It may be confusing to the desired person to experience this push-pull energetic.

The Romantic wishes to be met emotionally. Remember your own boundaries and cultivate clarity when you meet a Four's intensity. This will make it possible to honor the realm in which they live, without feeling pulled into a vortex of emotion. Listen and stay present with the Four, work on understanding rather than helping or changing them. Constancy and steadiness will help you deal with the push-pull energy.

The Gut Triad—Types Eight, Nine, and One

Eight, Nine, and One are the types that make up the gut center triad. The underlying emotion associated with the gut center is anger. It fuels the drive or passion for each of these gut types.

Straight Shooter Eight
Triad: Gut
Emotion: Anger externalized

Drive: Lust
Energy: Larger than life

Eight represents the externalized version of anger. The Straight Shooter's anger is like a summer thunderstorm: it rises quickly, booms and pounds intensely, and is over in a flash. When it's finished, it's finished. The air is clear.

Eight's drive or passion plays out as excess or lust. (Lust in this instance refers to a "lust for life" rather than sexual appetite.) Live life to the fullest, and then go further. Taste it, eat it, smell it! Give it everything you've got. Hold nothing back!

So it's not surprising that the energy of Eights strikes the rest of us as large. Straight Shooters fill up a room energetically. We feel their will and strength as a large force field extending out from them, pushing ahead with their agenda. We can either feel energized or intimidated by this energy. Whichever we may feel, Eights want to be met energetically.

Sensing from the gut, they push the force field out to check your force field. They want to know where you stand: Are you friend or foe? Will you stand your ground? Are you worthy? If you are intimidated and flee (either actually or with your energy by withdrawing inside yourself), the Eight moves forward. You may be foe or unworthy, and since the Eight can't sense your presence, they must move forward to confront, to find out what you're really made of.

As Caitlin, an Eight flight attendant describes her experience: "When people pull back from me or I can't get a sense of them, it feels like there's a 'power void' and I must move into it. I realize this now and I'm working on just allowing the void, but my natural reaction is to fill up the space." Nature abhors a vacuum, and no type exemplifies this more than Straight Shooter Eights.

To honor the Eight, we need to meet their considerable energy. To do this, we need to push our own energy from our gut. Bring your attention to the belly center. Now push out your own force field. Allow their force field to probe and find you. If you are trying to communicate with an Eight, be clear, direct, to the point. Don't be wishy-washy, don't explain your entire thinking process, just let 'er rip. Stand your ground while pushing out with your own force field. Do not escalate the conflict or discussion—this will just cause the Eight's energy to rise. Unless you are an Eight, you can't rise as far as they can and you'll be crushed. By the same token, do not wimp out or withdraw your energy. State your position clearly, firmly, and briefly while pushing out with your force field. Show yourself to be worthy of respect in the world of the Eight.

Mediator Nine

Triad: Gut
Emotion: Anger forgotten
Drive: Sloth or indolence
Energy: Diffuse extension

Nines have lost awareness of or forgotten they are angry, but they are no less driven by it than are Ones and Eights. Anger is kept safely hidden from the Mediator's view, but they pay a price by also losing their own priorities, desires, even their passion. The strength and action that are the birthright of the gut center are simply not felt. Nines are like an inactive volcano. It takes a lot of energy *not* to notice something, which may help explain why Nines often feel "low energy" or that they are enlivened by the energy of others.

Their drive is sloth or indolence toward their own priorities or agendas. Down in the Mediator Nine's gut lives not only forgotten anger, but also passion, life force, and a Nine's own desires and needs. This inadvertent sacrifice has Nines seemingly blowing whichever way the wind blows, just going along with life, rather than actively participating and creating a life.

Nines seem diffuse energetically to the rest of us, as if the molecules of their force field are spread out over a great distance. They passively sense their environment from the gut center and take in energy and cues from their surroundings and others. Their energy and attention can extend over a large area. One Mediator told me "I sometimes feel I can sense what is going on on the whole property, even though I'm in the front office."

Their feeling of being merged or "one with everything" can leave the rest of us wondering if they have a separate self or preference. They appear to just go along. If pushed hard however, they seem to sweetly solidify into a smiling immovable object. While they haven't chosen a course of action, they have rejected being pushed into one. We find them to be calm, peaceful, easygoing folk, albeit a little extended into the environment. Being with a Nine can feel like falling into a big, comfortable space.

Perfectionist One

Triad: Gut
Emotion: Anger internalized
Drive: Resentment
Energy: Rigid containment

One contains the internalized version of anger—resentment. Anger is stuffed deep inside and seeps out in the guise of irritation, frustration, and resentment. Perfectionists even turn anger against themselves in the form of haranguing by the internal critic. In this sense, Ones' anger is more like an active volcano that is not allowed to blow. Small bursts of steam vent through clenched teeth as the One seethes.

Resentment is the drive or passion of the Perfectionist One—small wonder, since anger doesn't get blown off as with the Eight. Ones are angry at *having* to circumvent their own desires for that which should be done. Furthermore, there doesn't seem to be any reward for being virtuous and responsible. One is angry at the inherent unfairness of this situation. Others just skate by, shirking responsibility or cutting corners, and they aren't penalized for it. In fact, others seem to be enjoying pleasure and indulging their desires, without necessarily having earned them.

The other eight points of the Enneagram experience the Perfectionist's energy as contained, but intense. (Pragmatic clarity and seriousness characterize Ones, when not angry.) There is a sense that if One did blow, it would be along the lines of Krakatoa. Sometimes, the energy can feel stabbing—like a small slice by the force field with each vent of steam, in the form of criticism. We can find ourselves on the defensive and pushing back angrily.

To meet One's energy, focus your attention on your belly and the ground. Keep your force field constant. Rather than get defensive, explain your position clearly and calmly. Take Ones seriously, and above all don't criticize them. Remember their inner critic is already bashing them.

One's energy can be rigid, tight when change is called for. Allow time if possible for the One to adjust to the change. While staying in your gut, point out that there is more than one right answer, and elicit their help with the change whenever possible.

Discovering Type Through Energy

Perhaps you recognize acquaintances, friends, and family from the descriptions of their energy or force fields. It may even have been easier to find their Enneagram type via energy than the descriptions of external and internal terrain. Taken together, these two parts of the map (energy and terrain descriptions) help us to discover another's type and worldview.

It may be more difficult for us to be aware of our own energy. After all, we're experiencing it from the inside rather than receiving its effect on the outside. It may be helpful to ask family and close friends how they experience us, to get a fuller picture of how our energy might specifically be perceived by others. That will give us more data than the general information about energy and type we've explored above.

Accessing Our Intelligence

While each of us has access to all three centers, the majority of us do not access all of them with equal ease. Depending on our Enneagram type, one center is our primary way of taking in and decoding information about the world. One of the remaining two centers (and it can be either) will be our secondary or support center. The last will be our tertiary or least utilized center.

Ideally we would like to have access to all three centers' intelligence in daily life. We'd like to be able to use our head, heart, and gut consciously in our decision making. Remember how all three intelligences were used in our hypothetical decision of a place to live? Our visionary and emotional intelligences complement each other, enabling us to make fully informed life choices.

How do we exercise our intelligences so that we can call upon them when needed? Through a simple awareness practice, we can awaken our intelligences and make them more accessible to us.

Exercise: Tapping Into the Three Centers

Close your eyes or let your gaze go soft and unfocused. Draw your attention inside yourself. Bring your attention to the head or visionary center, located just behind your eyes. Remember that this is the center of logical and abstract thought, language, imagery, and symbols—the center of planning and memory, of our dreams and imagination. This is the center of our visions of the future. Take a moment to notice how it feels in the head center. Is it comfortable or uncomfortable? Are there feelings, sensations, thoughts associated with it? Are there colors or shapes? Just notice.

Now shift your attention to the heart center, located right in the middle of your chest. Remember that this is the center of connection—to self and other beings. This is the center of relatedness, of empathy and compassion. It is from the heart that we know how others perceive us. Our emotional life lives here—love and loss, pain and bliss, longing and gratitude. Take a moment to notice how it feels in the heart center. Is it comfortable or uncomfortable? Are there feelings, sensations, thoughts associated with it? Are there colors or shapes? Just notice.

Now shift your attention to the gut center, located just below your umbilicus. Remember that this is the center of instinct, of gut knowing. This is the center of our strength and our will. Impulse and passion live here. This is the sensate center, where we *sense* where power lives, friend vs foe. This is the center of action and balance, and connection to the ground of the earth. Take a moment to notice how it feels in the gut center. Is it comfortable or uncomfortable? Are there feelings, sensations, thoughts associated with it? Are there colors or shapes? Just notice.

At first, one or more centers may be difficult to access. You may feel strange or uncomfortable—even in your primary center as delineated by your Enneagram type. That is perfectly normal. We may have shut down or avoided a particular center due to discomfort, social conditioning, or a painful event. It may simply be that we have rarely used it. With practice, we can gain equal access to all three centers and their intelligences.

Cami, a Performer Three, found she felt most comfortable in her heart, and secondly in her gut, when engaged in the centers practice. Her head "hurt" and felt tight and constricted to her. She felt like she "didn't want to be there." She related that it often took all her concentration to read street signs or a map to arrive at a destination. She found it easier to "feel" her way there. After a few months of working with the practice, she was surprised to find that one day her head center felt open, spacious, and very comfortable. She felt equally at ease in all three centers and marveled at how she just "worked better" after that. And she continued with her practice.

If we perform this simple awareness practice once or twice a day, we'll find that we seem to have more access to our various intelligences. They've always been there, but now we are cultivating them. Most of us have strengthened our mental muscles, but may still need work on the visionary aspect of our head center. In our culture, we may be very aware of how others perceive us, yet be out of touch with our own heart and emotions. We may be very good at sensing strength and power, yet need practice in allowing and accessing gut knowing. Even our primary center may have aspects we have not utilized. As we become more facile with our energy center practice, we find we may embrace the gifts each has to offer.

CHAPTER 4

The Dynamic Enneagram

I am often asked if one's Enneagram type changes. Certainly we grow and change as individuals, adopting more of the full spectrum of human potential as we gain life experience, whether or not we have the Enneagram map at our disposal. Yet our core personality or default mode seems to remain constant. While we can change behaviors, and some of our attitudes, our central worldview seems to stay with us.

Our "personal paradigm," if you will, describes reality for us—and reality doesn't change when we are convinced there truly is an *objective reality*. Everything we see or notice seems to bear out our version of reality—the worldview of our Enneagram type. And yet, there are times in our lives when we notice that we feel, act, and think very differently from our "normal" selves. What is happening at these times?

Putting the Map in Motion

The Enneagram is a dynamic map that describes not only our basic personality, but also how we seem to change under conditions of stress or conditions of security and ease. We actually move on the Enneagram diagram in predictable directions to take on aspects of another point or type.

Reaction to Stress

Our initial reaction to stressors is to exaggerate our normal behavior. We *become*—almost archetypally—our core points. Our usual way of perceiving and being has helped us cope in the past, and we call on our default mode to help us deal with the stress.

If our default mode is unsuccessful in alleviating the stress, we then move on the Enneagram diagram to access the energies and traits of another point. While we do not become this point or truly change our internal worldview, we can look and feel like our stress point. The arrows on the Enneagram diagram show to which point each type moves (see Figure 4-1). As you can see, type One, the Perfectionist, moves to Four; type Four, the Romantic, moves to Two, etc.

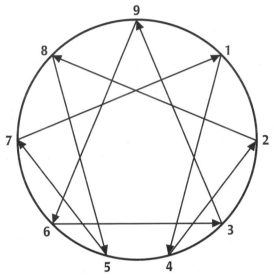

Figure 4-1 *Movement on the Enneagram in the direction of stress points.*

Response to Security

When in a situation of comfort or at ease, we may naturally access the energies of our comfort point or security point. The arrows in the diagram below show the point to which each type moves when comfortable or secure (see Figure 4-2). Type One moves to Seven, Seven moves to Five, etc. Again, we don't actually become this point or change our true internal terrain. We simply take on aspects and characteristics of this other type.

Knowing the energies we naturally access allows us a greater range of possibilities in our perceptions, actions, feelings and thoughts. As with our core Enneagram type, there is a high and low side to each of the energies we access. Our stress point is not necessarily "bad" and our comfort point is not necessarily "good." They are simply responses to

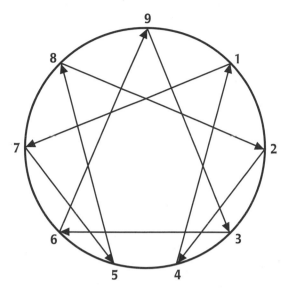

Figure 4- 2 *Movement on the Enneagram in the direction of security points.*

the dynamic circumstances in our lives. We may access the high or low
side of either. Stress is not necessarily bad. It may simply be a call for
new action, and our stress point can add new energies for that action.
Comfort situations may elicit a paradoxical reaction in us.

For example, retirement or vacation may be situations in which we
access the low side of our security point, even though we expect to be
at ease. We'll not be able to have much say in whether we access the
high or low side of these points if we remain unaware of how our personality type works. With consciousness and observation, we increase
our ability to access the high side of all the points toward which we
gravitate naturally.

Movement Under Stress—the Nine Types in Their Own Words

In this section, we'll examine the movement of each of the types
under conditions of stress. This movement follows the direction of the
arrows in the Enneagram diagram (see Figure 4-1). To underscore each
type's dynamic, we will look at the types as they follow these arrows,
beginning with the Perfectionist One.

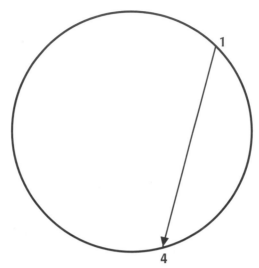

Figure 4-3 *Reacting to stress, the Perfectionist One moves to its stress point—Romantic Four.*

Perfectionist One

When overwhelmed, Perfectionists take on some of the energy and traits of the Romantic Four point. Of course, the One does not become a Four. They simply experience some of the traits of that type. They may find themselves longing for an idealized person or situation that will make everything complete in their life. Most Ones relate they pull inward when contacting the Four point, feeling melancholic and emotional, even depressed. A focus on inner life and feelings can keep the One from accomplishing as much as they usually do, further activating the inner critic.

This low side of Four is addressed by a Perfectionist:

> "For a long time, I thought I was a Four," muses Karla. "I suffered melancholy and longed for a perfect love to make my life wonderful. But when I listened to panels [a method of teaching also known as the Oral Tradition Enneagram™ developed by Helen Palmer, in which groups of each type speak about their 'internal terrain' and worldview for the purpose of instruction] of Ones and Fours, I realized that I did not find the melancholy bittersweet as did the Fours. I wanted to be done with it. My internal critic kept goading me with 'Aren't you over this yet?'

"When I saw the Ones, I realized the most driving force in my life has been the drive to be 'good'—and that my internal critic has harangued me for as long as I can remember. It now seems so obvious to me that I was literally living in my stress point when I was going through a painful divorce and life changes. Although it was hard, I suppose I needed to be in Four then."

Touching deep inner emotional territory is an aspect of the high side of Four for the Perfectionist Ones who surrender to it. Creativity and a rich inner life are benefits of the Romantic's point, and can be very nurturing to the Perfectionist if they don't get caught up in longing for the idealized person or thing.

Penelope, an artist, finds that she explores the deep emotional feelings of Four in her studio:

"The feelings go into my paintings. I feel that I truly can find some truth in exploring my depths, even if it is sometimes painful. I feel rejuvenated and alive after spending time working visually with my interior life. It offers me riches beyond belief. And the critic has very little to say about it, because my feelings are my feelings: They don't need fixing. Plus they have something important to offer me in my growth."

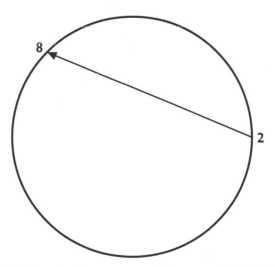

Figure 4-4 *Reacting to stress, the Giver Two moves to its stress point—Straight Shooter Eight.*

Giver Two

When stressed—which often occurs when the Twos have given until they are empty—Givers take on the energy of Eight. The low side rears its head as the Two blows up at others, bludgeoning them with their newfound boundaries. The Giver can seem overly controlling to those they usually help and please.

Sandra, a warm and caring Two, shares what happens when she is stressed:

> "When I am overwhelmed, it's like Mount Vesuvius going off. I just explode. My family tells me that it feels like it comes out of nowhere. I'm usually so caring and accommodating, but when I feel taken advantage of or unappreciated, look out. No one is safe. Later I feel emotionally drained and ashamed."

The high side of the Straight Shooter Eight involves clarity and a balanced sense of the Giver Two's own desires and boundaries.

Julie co-hosts a radio program on loving relationships:

> "I feel like I have been spending much more time in Eight, consciously. It is clear to me what I want and I'm much better at giving it to myself. I am better able to make decisions than when I wanted to please everyone else. When I give to others now, it feels like a choice rather than it being my only mode."

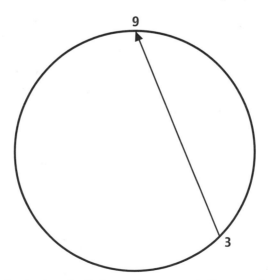

Figure 4-5 *Reacting to stress, the Performer Three moves to its stress point—Mediator Nine.*

Performer Three

Under conditions of stress, the Three moves on the diagram to the Nine point. Most Threes describe the low side of Nine as a place of paralysis: The doer is unable to accomplish. While the Three may remain in motion as is his modus operandi, nothing seems to get done. Nonessential things are attended to while important tasks are put off or ignored. The Three is unable to prioritize or make decisions. This paralysis is very uncomfortable for the goal-oriented Performer, who may be helpless to pull out of it.

Here's how Sam, a Performer Three, describes the low side of the Mediator Nine point:

> "I find myself very busy, making calls and working on projects as busily as I do normally. However, I find that I don't make the two really important calls that I needed to make, nor do I work on the projects that need my immediate attention. I somehow seem unable to direct my attention to what really needs to be done. I can't seem to focus but rather I find myself in chaos—activity without purpose, motion without accomplishment. Nothing is really getting done."

This sounds like a nightmare for the goal-directed Performer. But in fact, this can be a very important regrouping opportunity for the "go for it" Three. If the Performer realizes how the Mediator state of being can help reduce overwhelming stress, then the high side becomes more accessible and not just a happy accident.

The high side of Nine allows the Three to see the value in stopping for a time and floating downstream, rather than constantly pushing the oars—in being rather than accomplishing. The Performer discovers joy and purpose in surrendering to life's flow when they pursue this aspect of the Nine point and take time to contemplate what is important to them. They may find some of the Mediator's faith that life just works out when left to its own devices, that you don't have to make it happen.

Lyle, another Three, tells us:

> "I've found the high side of the Nine point most frequently when I've been out in nature. I feel no need to do or accomplish—it seems important to just appreciate the beauty before me. It is so clear that all this magnificence would happen

whether I showed up to see it or not. I feel like I blend with the scene around me and I am happy just existing in the moment."

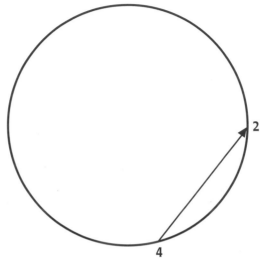

Figure 4-6 *Reacting to stress, the Romantic Four moves to its stress point—Giver Two.*

Romantic Four

When stressed the Romantic Four accesses energy of the Two point, the Giver. Fours can find themselves giving to others as a way of staving off abandonment and ensuring their importance to others. The low side of Two may show up as manipulating to ensure connection.

Cynthia lived in community at the farm. Normally self-sufficient and comfortable with solitude and quiet, she found herself acting in quite a different manner when her husband left for business travel:

"I would suddenly feel very needy, rejected, and concerned about abandonment. So I would be extra-giving and overly so-licitous toward my closest female friend. I would even find myself flattering her as a way of ensuring that she would stay connected to me, of guaranteeing that she wouldn't leave me. Looking back, I can see that I was not aware I was doing this, though I sensed that I was acting very differently from normal. Yet my friend always noticed and asked me point-blank what was going on.(She's an Eight!) I couldn't articulate it then, but I now see it as the low side of Two."

The high side of the Giver Two has the normally self-referencing Four looking outward to what others need and working to provide for them. The needs of others take precedence over the Four's interior and emotional life for a change while she attends to their wants.

Sela finds she is often stressed when she co-teaches photography and spirituality workshops with her husband, Brad. A very talented photographer and producer, she finds herself focusing on the workshop participants' comfort and well-being:

> "As if I didn't have enough to do with getting my materials and course content ready, I find myself divining discomfort among each of the participants. I suddenly 'knew' that one man needed a better pillow and rushed off to find a goose-down pillow for him. Another woman seemed uncomfortable staying in a cabin by herself and I moved her into a room with others. I find myself mothering and nurturing others almost naturally. Ordinarily, I assume most people can ask if they want something and then we can get it. In my stress position, I find myself seeking out others' needs and jumping in to fill them. I actually enjoy it, strangely enough. It pulls me out of my normal internally focused self."

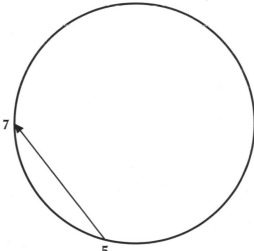

Figure 4-7 *Reacting to stress, the Observer Five moves to its stress point—Optimist Seven.*

Observer Five

When stressed, Observers access the Seven point and can find themselves drawn to multiple options and possibilities, frittering away their time and energy in the process. Fives may find themselves the life of the party, entertaining others. The energy boost and high excitement that the Optimist Seven provides can lead them to excess with alcohol, food, sex, etc.

Jon, a musician who performs in clubs on a regular basis, relates:

> "The only way I could seem to get up on stage was to access the Seven mode. I'm a pretty quiet, shy person ordinarily, but when I get on a stage I'm funny and witty and love performing. I would be so 'pumped up' by the end of the evening though, that I couldn't turn the energy off and would go home with the nearest willing female. I also drank to excess to quiet the energy down. Now I just watch the Seven energy, go home at the end of the night, unplug my phone, and watch old movies until the energy subsides."

The high side of Seven allows the Five to come out—to move toward instead of withdrawing and observing. Observers can be true "fun hogs" and great storytellers, enjoying performing and the spontaneity of play. The Optimist point offers another positive attribute to the Observer: an ability to see multiple options and possibilities.

Cathie shares her experience of buying a house:

> "All seemed to be moving along beautifully, until the lender reappraised the house for $9,000 less than the previous appraiser. I couldn't get the loan amount I needed to close the deal and the sellers wouldn't budge on price, despite the new appraisal. At the same time, I was selling my old house and had already closed the deal.
>
> "At first I could see no way out of my dilemma, other than to have no house and move into an apartment. This option was repugnant to me. As I became more stressed, options started occurring to me and I called friends, agents, and others to help me explore them. I could negotiate the return of my old house, get new loans, even move out of the area to a whole new environment. In the Seven mode, the possibilities seemed endless.
>
> "After exploring all the alternatives, I ultimately decided to go ahead and buy the house after all, with a personal loan to cover the extra $9,000. Examining my options gave me the freedom to make the decision I really wanted."

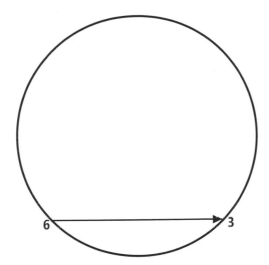

Figure 4-8 *Reacting to stress, the Loyal Skeptic Six moves to its stress point—Performer Three.*

Loyal Skeptic Six

When feeling overwhelmed, the Six moves to the Three point, using frenetic activity as a cure for stress. "If I just keep moving and doing, the stress is bound to be alleviated," the Loyal Skeptic thinks. When the Six is in action, fear falls away.

Maya, a cook at a retreat center, finds that serving a large group for a week is a challenge that pushes her right into the Performer point:

> "Even when everything is organized and the participants are delighted with the meal, I continue to cook, change recipes, bake bread, etc. far into the night. My companion complains I won't take a break to go for a walk or a swim, even when it is my scheduled time off. But I just feel more comfortable if I keep working. Afterward though, I'm often exhausted."

Some Sixes relate that they also become concerned with image—whether they appear to others as successful, important, etc. They may even find themselves shifting, adapting themselves to enhance their external image.

The high side of Three results when the Loyal Skeptic Six notices the value of forging ahead and doing. Analysis paralysis is no longer an issue as energy is transferred from the mental realm of anxiety to the physical realm of action. This aspect of the Performer actually allows

Sixes to overcome their usual aversion to success and act on their own behalf.

Anne describes her experience of the high side of Three as a feeling of getting mobilized, and getting past panic:

> "I feel like I shift into a place of action and direction. I move forward with a sense of purpose and clarity toward specific goals. In my younger days, I think I just moved into perpetual motion without a clear direction. It felt so good just to stop the fear. However, now my action is focused, and I make sure to add balance with two days a week that are my 'down days,' where I don't take any action. I rejuvenate myself so I don't fall prey to the low side of Three—just doing and doing and doing. I really enjoy the high side of Three and feel better about myself now."

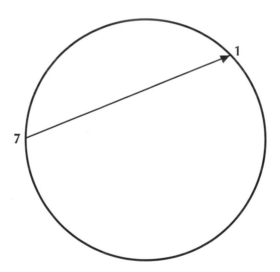

Figure 4-9 *Reacting to stress, the Optimist Seven moves to its stress point–Perfectionist One.*

Optimist Seven

When stressed, the playful Sevens access the energy of the Perfectionist. They may become critical of themselves and others, concerned with minor details, and fixated on what is "right." Our Optimist can become rigid and inflexible, resentful of others who aren't pulling their weight.

The author describes how it plays out for her:

"I am a laissez-faire housekeeper at best. I generally keep things 'clean enough to be healthy and messy enough to be happy.' Yet under stress, I find myself scouring sinks and countertops that are already clean. I even line up the kitchen sponge equidistant to the hot and cold faucets. Nothing seems good enough. I find myself 'irritated' by my messy family and muttering through clenched jaws: 'Nobody ever cleans up around here. What a bunch of pigs.'

"I now recognize this as a sign that I am stressed. The family hasn't changed—I have. Suddenly I am rigid, judgmental, and frustrated. I've moved to the One point. I need to alleviate my stress and take care of myself before it spills over onto them."

One energy can help the Optimist focus and get organized. When clarity emerges from chaos, accomplishment starts to take precedence over this Seven's normal preoccupation with process:

"More often these days, I find myself accessing the high side of One. I'll feel tense, the house will look messy, and I'll head straight to my office. There I set to work organizing, filing, and finishing half-completed projects. I take delight in how perfect I can make something and enjoy my accomplishment. I feel clear and focused as I work through my own inner chaos by moving to the One point."

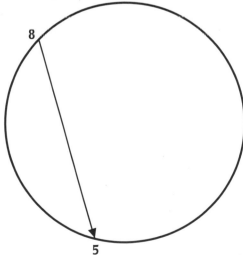

Figure 4-10 *Reacting to stress, the Straight Shooter Eight moves to its stress point–Observer Five.*

Straight Shooter Eight

When stressed, the decisive person-of-action retreats into the Five point, pulling away from intrusion, sequestering themselves inside the castle, courting invisibility. The Observer's thinking replaces Eight's characteristic doing.

Chris commands a Marine regiment. He is a larger-than-life Eight used to making split-second decisions and being in control. Under a tremendous amount of stress, he found himself living in Five:

"We were on maneuvers and I was just exhausted. I remember lying in my sleeping bag, looking up at a pine tree overhead. My greatest ambition in life at that moment was to be a pine nut, tucked in with all the other little pine nuts, where no one could see me. Realizing this, I thought something was seriously wrong with me."

Learning the Enneagram gave Chris the map he needed to understand that he was not going crazy. He was simply a normal Straight Shooter Eight experiencing an overload of stress. A succession of hundred-hour weeks had simply taken their toll, proving even a strong, energetic Eight has limits. He allowed himself time to rest and rejuvenate, and abandoned his desire to become a "pine nut."

The high side of Five gives Eight a break, much like the Nine point does for the Three. The Straight Shooter gets a chance to think things through before making decisions, to value analysis and a slower pace. Pulling energy in rather than filling up all the space leaves more of it available to the Eight.

Lowell, a Straight Shooter Eight vice president of a large investment firm, asserts:

"I have no trouble seeing that I've accessed Five many times. I've always thought of myself as a closet intellectual. At times, I like to pull back a little, to think and muse on ideas. I'll read great thinkers and ponder ways to incorporate their ideas into my decisions and actions. I like ideas, but not just as mental constructs. I want to find ways to apply them. Then they are of practical use to me."

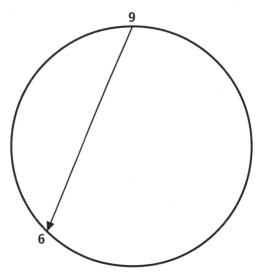

Figure 4-11 *Reacting to stress, the Mediator Nine moves to its stress point–Loyal Skeptic Six.*

Mediator Nine

Under stress, the easygoing Mediator accesses the anxiety and worry of the Six point. Temporarily losing the faith that ordinarily sustains them on a daily basis, the Nine worries and suffers from worst-case-scenario imaginings. Like the Loyal Skeptic Six, the Nine can begin to look for clues in the environment that support their extremist visions.

Jenna believes she has truly accessed Six only once in her life—when she lost her job:

> "Worried about my financial survival, I experienced a general feeling of anxiety and impending doom that lasted for three weeks while I searched frantically for employment. But there was another, stranger development.

> "I was living in the San Francisco Bay area at the time, and during this three-week period I suffered from an acute fear of driving over bridges. I would envision the bridge collapsing and my car falling into the water below, trapping and drowning me. The mental imagery would be so vivid as I drove over the bridges that I would pull over to the side, shaking and white-knuckled. There I would wait until I felt I could continue across.

> "After three weeks, I landed a good job and the fear of driving across bridges vanished. To this day, I have not had a recurrence."

On the high side, anxiety can push the Nine toward Loyal Skeptic Six and right into action. And worst-case scenario thinking can galvanize the Mediator into planning ahead. Instead of allowing life to happen, Nines can find themselves looking ahead to the future and taking action to effect results.

John, a twenty-two-year-old Nine finds the high side of Six when he has let important projects go until the last moment:

> "Worst-case scenarios cascade through me, and I see myself out on the street with no food, no job, no home. I roar into action, chart how to complete the project, and get down to business. I see the possible pitfalls inherent in the project as if they were happening, and it is easy for me to make a plan to deal with them. It feels so different from my usual mode of being. I hate being scared, but it seems to serve a useful purpose—and it energizes me."

Movement With Security—the Nine Types in Their Own Words

Our security point may also be called the "point of evolution" (Riso calls it "integration") because we seem to access it more as we live longer. Perhaps as we get older, we just naturally get a little more comfortable with ourselves.

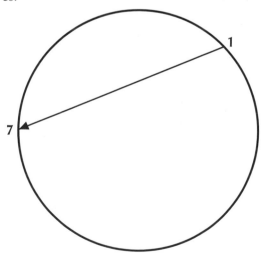

Figure 4-12 *Responding to security, the Perfectionist One moves to its security point—Optimist Seven.*

Perfectionist One

The move to Seven is a joyful expansive place for most Ones. Most often accessed on vacations or away from day-to-day responsibilities, the Perfectionist's playful child emerges. They enjoy life and all its delights and possibilities. In short, they have fun.

Danielle is a responsible, dependable One. She tends to be serious and hardworking around home and office. Yet she is a self-described "fun hog" when on vacation:

"I went to Bali and just sampled the sights, the food, the people. I had a wonderful time. I laughed and danced and played. While there, I met a man from my hometown and we went out together several times. Since we had such a great time, we made plans to get together after returning home.

"When we went out again, we didn't link up at all, nor did we have a good time. He told me I didn't seem like the same person he'd met in Bali and I knew what he meant, though it upset me. I was home again—responsible, serious, no longer in my Seven point. And while I love the freedom of Seven, I also like my One bent toward improvement and the serious work in life. I can't change that—and I don't want to."

The low side of the Optimist Seven is often referred to as the "trap-door." Perfectionist Ones can deny themselves pleasure for so long in the service of "shoulds," that they literally explode into hedonistic episodes. They "fall through the trapdoor." Later, self-recrimination has Ones promising themselves they'll never do anything so "wrong" again. Not all Ones experience the trapdoor, but most find that exploration of multiple options and possibilities can keep the One as unfocused as an unconscious Seven.

Susanne finds the low side of Seven manifests in her hobbies. She tries a little of everything and feels that she is not very good at any one thing. She finds herself getting bored and moving on to a new diversion or craft continually:

"I like to sew, but don't always finish what I start. I'm been involved in photography, basket making, piano playing, gardening, stamping and embossing, cooking, cross-stitch, and the list goes on. I definitely feel like the dilettante when I try everything but don't finish or stay with it. I feel very focused in

my work and other projects, but am almost flighty when it comes
to my hobbies. It's like I have the attention span of a gnat.
Everything seems fun . . . for a little while. Then I'm off to
something new."

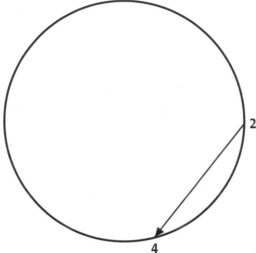

Figure 4-13 *Responding to security, the Giver Two moves to its security point—Romantic Four.*

Giver Two

The move to Four affords Giver Twos a mode for focusing their
attention inward to their own emotional life, rather than outward to
others' emotions and needs. Twos often relate that they find their own
creativity and authentic self-expression in exploring the realm of the
Romantic.

Susan finds it is important to her to have solitary time to feel her
own feelings, to explore her internal life:

"I have a hard time being internal when there is even one
other person in the room. I can't help but be aware of their
needs and concerns. When I'm alone, I can spend time with
my own emotional life. My sculpting and painting encourage
my looking inward, and give me an outlet for my emotions. I
am amazed at what I create—I am actually a very good artist.
Yet the reason I do it is not to be a 'good artist' but to make
sacred space for me, to explore who I am apart from the person
who 'helps others.'"

Accessing the low side of Four, Twos can become lost in longing for an idealized lover, job, or object that will complete them. In that case, they tend to indulge in melancholy and drama.

Betty had a well-paying job that afforded her respect and travel. Her husband and kids were accomplished, healthy, and loving. Yet she wasn't happy:

> "I felt that something essential was missing. At first, I thought it was romance. I felt that my husband wasn't intimate enough, that we should be sharing our deepest thoughts and feelings with each other. So he went into therapy and began trying to meet those needs.

> "Then it seemed to me it was the corporate world that made me unhappy. What I really needed to complete myself was to 'chuck it all' and go back to nature, live in a yurt and garden all day.

> "I kept focusing on a certain 'something' that would make it all work for me, make me happy. When I focused on something it was the only thing that would help. If only I had 'this' then my life would be perfect. Yet when 'this' was within my grasp, it no longer seemed desirable.

> "I've since found that I was lost in the low side of Four. I'm learning to be happy, but it isn't related to any of these things. Changing my lifestyle drastically or remaking my relationship isn't going to make me happy or complete. That's something that will have to come from inside me, and I'm working on it."

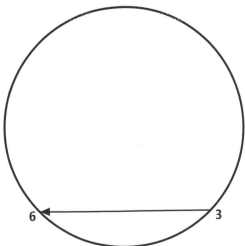

Figure 4-14 *Responding to security, the Performer Three moves to its security point—Loyal Skeptic Six.*

Performer Three

When comfortable or at ease, the Three accesses the energy of Six, the Loyal Skeptic. No longer needing to be in the spotlight, the Performer is content to work behind the scenes or put their talents for prodigious "doing" or selling in the service of some higher purpose. While exhibiting strong loyalty to causes or other people, Performer Threes may still engage in reasonable doubt, appropriate questioning, and caution.

Dewitt had been a highly successful photojournalist and seminar leader for years. He found himself searching for a new challenge, an occupation that would in his words "go beyond success to significance." He began to put his slides together to illustrate concepts of creativity and found himself on the lecture circuit, literally selling people their own creativity.

> "Most of us were talked out of ever believing we were creative, at a very early age. Based on lessons I learned shooting for National Geographic, I illuminate some very simple principles to remind people of their innate creativity and how they use it every day. My goal is to offer my contribution, then disappear at the end of my talk, like the Cheshire Cat from *Alice in Wonderland*, leaving only a smile."

The low side of Loyal Skeptic Six involves rampant worst-case scenario thinking and worry, causing Performers to become paralyzed by doubt and fear. Suspicion that other people harbor hidden motives may disrupt trust or relationships.

Dewitt had floated down the Colorado River through the Grand Canyon in wooden dories several times. Since he was conducting photo seminars, all the participants were his students. Often his wife and son accompanied him as well. On his tenth trip he went with some former students, friends, and his wife and son. Throughout the seventeen-day trip, he was plagued with worst-case scenario visions of his wife and son drowning, feelings of doom, and worries that "something terrible was going to happen." He recounts:

> "I rarely find myself experiencing the low side of Six. Yet despite my awareness that I indeed was caught up in Six-like catastrophic thinking I simply could not shake it. My anxiety was so strong at one point that I actually asked the trip leader

to put away the inflatable kayak that people were using to navi-
gate the smaller rapids. I explained to him that I just had a bad
feeling about it. He honored my fears and acquiesced. Nothing
happened on the trip, save some big storms and one boat flip.
But I was never so glad to get off the river. I'm not usually fearful, but this time, I simply could not relax."

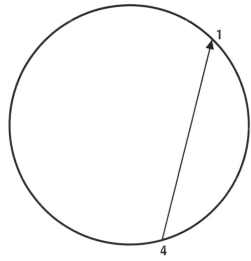

Figure 4-15 *Responding to security, the Romantic Four moves
to its security point—Perfectionist One.*

Romantic Four

The move to the Perfectionist is centering, focusing for Fours. Pulled
out of their rich internal emotional life, they engage in producing and
accomplishing. They are out in the world doing things well.

Alyssa produced a musical CD to accompany her multimedia slide
show showcasing Monument Valley, Arizona. She worked thirteen- to-
sixteen-hour days with the composer until she was satisfied:

> "I wanted it to be right. It needed not only to be done, but
> to be as perfect as we could make it. I focused on the details,
> fitting music to images. I wanted the people who commissioned
> the work to get our best efforts, to have a show they could be
> proud of."

Fours accessing One can become hypercritical and judgmental, sure
of their own "rightness." They can also lose the forest for the trees,
becoming focused on minutiae and obsessing over detail.

Heather, ordinarily a Romantic Four, was preparing for a seminar at the retreat center she hosts with her husband:

"Everything was ready and we had planned to get a good night's rest before our next group arrived. Instead, I found my-self staying up to work on these bamboo napkin rings I had been making, with Hawaiian expressions burned into them. It was exacting, demanding work and I was completely focused on completing them. I stayed up until 3:00 A.M., making them just perfect, choosing just the right inscriptions. As if anyone would notice whether we had napkin rings or not! We hadn't had them before, so probably didn't need them now.

"I can see this in retrospect, but at the time, it seemed criti-cal to attend to the details of the napkin rings, to do them just right. From a larger perspective, it is clear I would probably have served our guests better by being rested for their arrival."

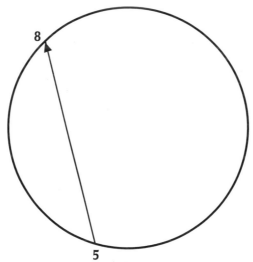

Figure 4-16 *Responding to security, the Observer Five moves to its security point—Straight Shooter Eight.*

Observer Five

Fives accessing the Straight Shooter's Eight point don't actually become larger than life or fill a room. But they do become assertive and express their viewpoint clearly and pointedly. Plus, they make expedi-ent decisions and act on them.

At her regular meeting of regional healthcare educators and train-
ers, Anna—an Observer Five organizational development
consultant—usually sat quietly at the table and summed up important
points when the meeting was over. At one point, Lynn, a Performer
Three, began to justify her position with a series of "facts." Anna was
familiar with the data Lynn was quoting:

> "She was playing fast and loose, misrepresenting the stud-
> ies and the facts, so I leaned forward, shook my finger in her
> face, and said, 'That is simply not true.' I then proceeded to
> clearly outline the true facts. Everyone at the table was stunned
> and I realized that I'd never reacted so clearly or strongly be-
> fore. And I loved it!"

Fives can access the low side of the Straight Shooter by becoming
excessively controlling. They sometimes become tyrants at home or in
the office.

As the successful publisher of several magazines, Stan has the repu-
tation of being overly controlling in the day-to-day operations of getting
out his publications. Although he has editors for each, all decisions
must be cleared through him. He has the final say on all material, ads,
etc.

> "I realize that sometimes we get backed up and my need for
> control slows the process down. I can't help feeling that I know
> best how the magazine should look and feel. I now realize I've
> lost some good editorial staff by not allowing them autonomy,
> and I'm trying to relinquish some control. But I find it very
> difficult."

Loyal Skeptic Six

When at ease or comfortable, the Six moves to the Nine point,
accessing the everpresent faith of Mediators that whatever happens,
it's all for the best. The Six relaxes into the flow of the present moment
and a trust that things do work out, even when we don't plan or worry.

Melissa, a Six therapist, relates that she nearly always accesses the
Nine point when going on vacation:

> "Usually, I plan everything and have a backup for every
> contingency. But when I'm going on a trip, I like to just go with
> the flow. I like having no plans and just wandering with no

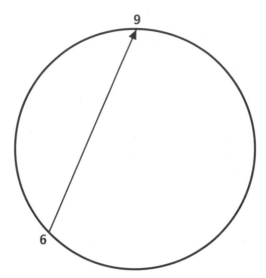

Figure 4-17 *Responding to security, the Loyal Skeptic Six moves to its security point—Mediator Nine.*

agenda. I don't worry about scheduling or timing or missing transportation (which drives my husband nuts). I really feel that everything will work out just fine and it always does."

The Six can find themselves a victim of circumstance by letting life just happen to them. This low side of the passive, go-with-the-flow Nine can keep the Six from accomplishing what they wish or taking control over their own destiny.

Katrina is a forty-two-year-old mother and homemaker. She describes the low side of Mediator Nine as it manifests for her:

"At times I just feel caught up by the flow of life, like I couldn't change it if I wanted. And at those times, it doesn't seem like it really matters what happens—like I don't have any say in the matter anyway. It feels like too much effort to 'push the river' and really engage. I may be doing a lot, but it doesn't feel like I have a choice. Life is just taking me along, like a leaf down a stream."

Optimist Seven

Sevens in Five find an internal life where they become interested in going very deeply into a subject or activity, rather than being dis-

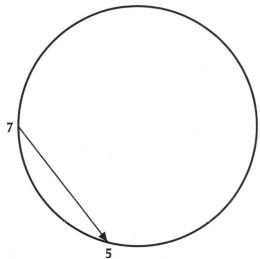

Figure 4-18 *Responding to security, the Optimist Seven moves to its security point–Observer Five.*

tracted an array of possibilities. They become focused and intent on becoming knowledgeable, even expert, in a particular realm.

Victoria is a multitalented Seven, involved in a number of pursuits. Yet once she began to study the Enneagram, she became single-minded in her focus to learn and experience all she could for her own personal growth. As she immersed herself in the Enneagram, her understanding grew and she found herself training to become a certified Enneagram teacher. Victoria eventually co-founded a business teaching the Enneagram, and has co-conducted ground-breaking research on intimacy and the instinctual subtypes:

> "I find that I keep learning as I explore and teach the Enneagram. In the beginning, I read voraciously and attended every class I could find. Now, as an Enneagram 'teacher,' I am committed to contributing to the knowledge available, for myself and for my peers and students. And it is true—I am more focused than I have ever been in my life."

The low side of Five can result in disengagement and retreat to the mental realm of ideas and knowledge. Like a true Observer, the Sevens can withdraw so much that they experience themselves as invisible and insubstantial. The author shares her experience:

"I spent a great deal of time in Five a couple of years after learning the Enneagram. I retreated to my home, reading and thinking, working on learning more. I socialized less and less and began to feel that I really didn't take up space anymore. I was nearly agoraphobic; I didn't want to leave the house even to get groceries. I remember standing in line at a store counter— I was next in line and the cashier looked past me to the person behind me and said, 'Next.' I truly felt invisible and knew I had to make an effort to re-engage my energy with the world, or I might risk simply disappearing altogether."

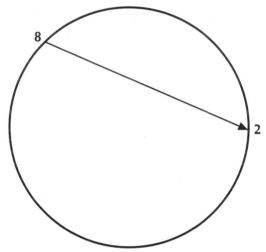

Figure 4-19 *Responding to security, the Straight Shooter Eight moves to its security point—Giver Two.*

Straight Shooter Eight

When moving to Two, Eights become interested in caring for others, realizing they have an impact on them. Beyond the Straight Shooter's usual protective stance, Eights in Giver Two are concerned with filtering decisions through the heart as well as the gut. They are interested in people's feelings, likely to sense others' needs and to act to help fill them.

Harold, a naval commander, was known as a decisive, strong, no-nonsense leader. In doing his job well, he sometimes trampled on others' feelings:

"When I found out that I actually hurt people, it was such a shock to me. What I did, I did to make sure my men were protected and to get the job done. It never occurred to me that I was upsetting people. Maybe at one time in my life, I wouldn't have cared. Now that I'm in my late fifties, it upsets me to upset others. I don't want to run roughshod over anyone when it isn't necessary. (I'll still do it if it is necessary!) I now examine what I say and how I react, to assess how it will be received. Since I really do care about the people I work, I think about the impact I have on them."

Eights can also access the low side of the Two point, becoming manipulative and giving to get. They can believe that they alone know what's good for another and "help" them to see it.

Marla is a financial consultant and mother of three. She shares her experience of the low side of the Giver Two:

"At first I would have said that I *never* give to get and *never* manipulate people. I am simply not like that. But my kids remind me that I have at times been the archetypal 'Jewish mother.' I give, expecting something in return—and dish out guilt when I don't get it! In trying to get them to do what I think is best for them, however, I push with Eight-like strength—way beyond that of a genuine Two."

Mediator Nine

When at ease, the Nine moves into Performer mode, gracefully doing and accomplishing. Mediators can be highly successful goal-directed achievers.

Ben is an artist who juggles art with running a small card business and taking part in community service projects:

"I can't wait to get up in the morning! I'm so excited, even passionate, about all I'm doing that I'm in a hurry to get started every day. I love accomplishing so much and I have to admit I enjoy being successful."

Obsessive doing may manifest as the low side of the Three point for Nines. Chameleon-like adaptations of the Performer style can find the Mediator on the slippery slope of self-deceit.

Tom is vice president of a major domestic air carrier. At one point, his family complained that he worked all the time. He'd travel for weeks

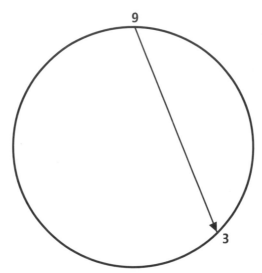

Figure 4-20 *Responding to security, the Mediator Nine moves to its security point–Performer Three.*

at a time. Then after returning home, he'd put in extra hours at the office and bring work home. He found himself identifying himself with his job. When confronted with his workaholic behavior, he says:

> "I appeared to be the caring husband and father, giving them whatever they wanted and fitting the image. But I really just wanted to get back to work. I also found myself letting people know about my accomplishments—telling them I'd been on CNN or featured in a national business magazine. I defined myself by my success."

In the process of discovering our Enneagram type, we often pick two or three types with which we resonate strongly. These types commonly include our core personality type, as well as our stress point and security point.

Observing how we behave when we are stressed can help lead us back to our core point. Of course, in the middle of stress, we may not be aware of how we are behaving, perceiving, or feeling differently. When the stress eases, however, we can look backward and notice how we were "different" from usual. Likewise, exploring the manifestations of our security point can help guide us home to our essential type.

Now let us explore two other points that aid us in determining our basic Enneagram type: "wing points."

Wings for the Nine Types

Each Enneagram type incorporates the energy of at least one of the two points next to it on the diagram. We call these points on either side "wings." For example, a One may have a Two wing or a Nine wing. While the worldview of Ones will determine their behaviors and traits, their personality will be "flavored" with Two-ish or Nine-ish behaviors and traits as well. If a One recognizes their basic personality is enhanced by Two, we say they are a One with a Two wing. If their personality is colored by some of the aspects of Nine, we say they have a Nine wing. If both Nine and Two equally flavor the One's basic personality, we say they are "bi-winged."

Most people have one wing point that is dominant, although at some point in life, they may access the energy from the other point. What is important is to recognize that the wings are additional energies we may easily draw upon, should we need them. Our wings are like "peripheral points" we can exercise and use when we most need the innate wisdom they offer.

In some cases, we can even overdevelop a wing point to disguise our natural personality so that we can get along in the world. This most often happens when we perceive that our real point or personality would not be acceptable to others. For example, a female Eight may not feel that her larger-than-life Eightness is acceptable at school, work, home, or anywhere. To get by in the world, she might overdevelop a Seven wing or Nine wing to "cover" her true identity. That is, she would show outwardly more of the Seven-ish or Nine-ish traits she naturally has access to, while keeping her internal worldview of Eight private. She would exhibit Optimist or Mediator qualities while still holding the beliefs and attention of an Eight inside.

Depending on our dominant wing, our energy and personality will be colored in a particular and observable way. A One with a Nine wing will appear quite different from a One with a Two wing. Here are some general descriptions about the flavoring of wings and how they differ. However, these are only generalizations and the wings are just another aspect of our internal terrain. As such, they may only be recognizable by and useful to the individual inhabiting this territory.

Perfectionist One

One With a Nine Wing

Ones who have Nine as their dominant wing tend to be thoughtful and measured in their speech patterns. They may seem outwardly calmer than Ones with Two wings. The stubbornness and procrastination of the Mediator may be accessory traits for the One with a Nine wing. They may mull over decisions for a time before making a commitment.

One With a Two Wing

Ones with a Two wing often have rapid speech tumbling out as if there are not enough hours in the day. Under the influence of the Giver, they make quick decisions, are helpful and caring, and share what they know to be best for others. Often they can sense what others need. (Unlike Twos, they don't necessarily feel compelled to provide the help others "need.")

Giver Two

Two With a One Wing

Concern with being dependable and responsible comes up for Twos with One wings, but it is still in service of being indispensable and important to those the Two cares for. Like Perfectionists, the Two may be focused on doing things "right," but again only for the approval of those important to them.

Two With a Three Wing

The Two with a Three wing often likes being center stage and has a double dose of the chameleon energy. Shapeshifting can be a way of life. Like the Performer, this Two can cut corners as long as the image looks good. This is where he differs from the Two with a One wing, who does things "right," if only for a select audience.

Performer Three

Three With a Two Wing

Although focused on recognition for personal achievement, the Three with a Two wing is often driven to help others achieve and succeed. Like the Giver with a Three wing, they have a double dose of the chameleon, adapting to what others want.

Three With a Four Wing

The Three with a Four wing often displays sensitivity or emotional intensity. Their Romantic tendency makes them more focused on image-crafting than actual accomplishing and doing. Although this is often internally sensed by the Three, to the rest of us, Threes seem to be accomplishing prodigious amounts. Feelings still may be put aside when they interfere with the task at hand.

Romantic Four

Four With a Three Wing

Accomplished and versatile, Fours with a Three wing tend to be outgoing and goal-oriented. They may also be overtly dramatic in their presentation and style of dress, showing a desire to be noticed, to be the center of attention. They are image-conscious, but do not wish to adapt as the Performer Three does: they must be unique, as well as successful.

Four With a Five Wing

Fours with a Five wing are just as concerned with uniqueness but less driven to be noticed. Flavored by the Observer point, their presentation and dress may be quietly different rather than overtly dramatic. Romantics with a Five wing are less likely to multitask and may spend significant amounts of time alone.

Observer Five

Five With a Four Wing

There is an attraction to the emotional realm when the Romantic colors the Observer. Fives with a Four wing describe times alone when they feel melancholy and longing. Feelings still feel safer when Fives can process and think about them by themselves.

Five With a Six Wing

The Five with a Six wing has a healthy dose of the Loyal Skeptic and may question authority, the status quo, etc. Fear can play a larger part for him. The Five with a Six wing can appear to be more cerebral than the Five with a Four wing.

Loyal Skeptic Six
Six With a Five Wing

The Five wing gives the Six a need for privacy and alone time. He may adopt the Observer role and compartmentalize time and energy. He can analyze and think things through interminably, if not careful.

Six With a Seven Wing

Sixes with a Seven wing have a more airy light energy than their Five wing counterparts. A desire for adventure and fun can override some of the usual Six caution, although they often still make contingency plans even for adventures. The Optimist wing point gives Six periodic bouts of optimism.

Optimist Seven
Seven With a Six Wing

Sevens with a Six wing tend to be more cautious, fearful, and doubting than those with an Eight wing. While still wildly optimistic, these Optimists flavored by the Loyal Skeptic can suddenly envision worst-case scenarios and be wary of hidden motives. Often, they use charm to disarm whomever or whatever appears frightening.

Seven With an Eight Wing

Sevens with an Eight wing tend to be bolder and more aggressive than those with a Six wing. Like the Straight Shooter, they may be fully engaged in exploring all life has to offer with little fear or reservation. They may be persuasive and assertive in pushing their agenda or idea, before they become bored and move on to another.

Straight Shooter Eight
Eight With a Seven Wing

Eights with a Seven wing are gregarious, outgoing, and jump into life with both feet. Excess (lust) and gluttony are a potent combination in these lust-for-life individuals. Moving fast, they work hard and play hard. Ideas fly and the Optimist-colored Eight has the energy to manifest them quickly—sometimes before they are fully thought out.

Eight With a Nine Wing

The Mediator Nine wing brings a slowing down and emphasis on harmony to the bigger-than-life Eight. They may enjoy merging with others and just being, rather than doing, for short periods of time. They may even play the Mediator in their family or organization, though they will still have much larger energy than the true Nine.

Mediator Nine

Nine With an Eight Wing

The Nine with a Straight Shooter Eight wing may find the energy to take a stand, be clear and direct, exert control, make decisions (such as at work as a boss or leader)—as long as it doesn't involve their personal agenda. They often continue to suffer the Nine's dilemma of difficulty acting on their own behalf.

Nine With a One Wing

The Nine with a Perfectionist One wing is likely to have strong feelings about what is right vs. wrong. They may take a strong stand when motivated by unfairness or social injustice, particularly when visited on others. On the other hand, if the unfairness involves the Nine themselves, they may not take a stand on their own behalf.

Gender Notes Regarding Wings

Male Twos

Our cultural image of masculinity does not honor the male Giver Two. A nurturing, caring, relationship-driven man is not perceived as the American ideal of success. (In fact, the Two is our feminine ideal.) Young male Twos quickly divine this fact, and most of them overdevelop the Perfectionist One or Performer Three wing as a way of working and coping in the world. They may be confused initially when learning the Enneagram, in attempting to discover their home base point. They may have been so successful at covering their Two worldview, they have hidden it from themselves. Fortunately, self-observation helps us find our true type soon enough.

Male Fours

Unless you are an artist, actor, or writer, our culture also does not honor the male Romantic Four. A sensitive, melancholy man longing for emotional intensity has no place in the U.S. workplace. Yet many male Fours are in all walks of life. They have coped by camouflaging themselves with their wing points of Performer Three or Observer Five. Like male Twos, some may confuse what their core point is, depending on how strongly developed the wing point is. Three men are an ideal in American business, and Five men are honored in many professions. These points are safe to "be" for a male Four.

Female Threes

The very attributes that American businesses have idealized in men are devalued in women. Happily, that is changing, albeit slowly. If a man multitasks, he is productive. A woman is scattered. A man is assertive and a go-getter; a woman is aggressive. U.S. culture likes its men ambitious, willing to work long hours, and goal-oriented. It likes women to be nurturing, caring, and feeling. Female Threes have often had to overdevelop the Giver Two wing (our feminine ideal) or the Romantic Four wing to fit in in all areas of our society. The adaptability of the Performer comes in very handy. Thankfully, it is becoming safer for the female Three to be "seen."

Female Eights

Eightness is far from our idea and ideal of femininity. Women are not larger than life, direct, decisive, warriors given to excess. In our culture, women are not Eights. While some very strong Straight Shooter Eight women have fought for societal recognition of who they are, many have worked to pull back their energy or channel it into more acceptable directions. While some Eight women have indeed overdeveloped the Optimist Seven or Mediator Nine wings as a way of fitting in, others have accessed the security point of the Giver Two, our 1950s ideal of true femininity. Thus many female Eights have often channeled their strength and energy into mothering protection and caretaking. Their inclination toward excess is still a factor to contend with, however.

This brief overview of wings is meant only to give a hint of how the points on either side of ours might flavor our personalities. As we observe ourselves, we learn how those influences play out for us individually. Noting the influences of our core point, our two wings, and our movement under stress and ease, we find we can fairly easily access the energy of five of the nine Enneagram points. Ideally, we would like to access the high side or most functional aspects of each of the points we touch. The key to working with ourselves, to living up to our full potential starts with the key to self-development: self-observation.

CHAPTER 5

A Map for Personal Growth and Self-Mastery

When you try to understand everything, you will not understand anything. The best way is to understand yourself, and then you will understand everything.

—Shunryu Suzuki

Imagine you have lived in Idaho for your entire life. You've never traveled more than 30 miles from home. You are told to go to Florida. You didn't do all that well in geography in school, but you have a vague idea that it is southeast. Can you imagine making your way there—without a map? It would be an enterprise of trial and error—total guesswork! You might take highways headed south and east, but it would still entail a great deal of time and zigzagging before you arrived where you wanted to be. To plot a course to any destination—you have to start by finding out where you are now. Ideally, you'll use a map to establish your current position, as well as where you'd like to end up.

Traveling our internal terrain is no different (except that few of us had a class in inner geography in school.) We humans are mostly uncharted territory. The Enneagram offers a map to find our starting place and help us plot a course to where we would like to be—where we become more whole as human and spiritual beings. Most of us have managed to grow and evolve, whether or not we had the Enneagram or another framework. We certainly learn through trial and error methodology, but how much more helpful it is to have a map, so we know not only where we are going but also how far we've come—to measure our progress.

To Know Yourself, Start From Where You Are

Our Enneagram personality type is home base. We begin our life's journey relatively unconscious of the programming of our personality; of our point on the map. As we become more aware of the ways in which our worldview colors reality for us, we are less likely to remain strictly at our starting point. We strike out on the journey to experience other worldviews, other colors in the spectrum of human potential. And as with our hypothetical trip to Florida, a map is invaluable to our travels.

Melissa had spent years working on her personal growth and her inner life:

> "As an artist, I felt it was important to me to know as much about myself as possible. I did Yoga, psychosynthesis, meditation retreats, all kinds of things. Yet there were times when I wondered if all my hard work really made any difference. When I learned the Enneagram, I found that I could actually see not only where I began as an unconscious One, but how I have changed. As a 'good' One, I was interested in continually improving myself. Now I find that I see many more shades of gray and am less judgmental with myself and others. I can actually see that all the work I had done had helped me with my 'Oneness.' And that is a great gift to me."

Like all maps, the Enneagram can only be a direction finder—a guide. We must do the actual traveling ourselves. To truly move, we must *experience* our inner life. A map of Florida does not convey the experience of baby-powder sand, balmy breezes, azure ocean, mangrove tangled swamps, flat landscape, etc. We must be present—use the map, then go beyond it to truly experience the place—whether it be Florida or our own inner landscape.

Then Decide Where You're Going

Once we determine our type and find our point on the Enneagram map, how then do we work with that knowledge? Where are we going? We want to experience more of our gift and grow into our best selves.

We also want to access more of the spectrum of human potential, so that we are not limited by the restrictive worldview of our personality type. The Enneagram map accurately describes these destinations for us.

The map is not the territory, therefore the real exploration is up to us. Six invaluable steps assist us along our journey. They are simple, but they are not easy. It will take clear intention and attention to carry out the real work of exploring our internal landscape. Yet it promises to be the most rewarding excursion you will ever embark upon.

Step One: Self-Observation

Self-observation is the key to determining our Enneagram point. It is also the key to heightening our awareness of our personality's default mode. Each of the nine personality types fixates attention in an unconscious or habitual way. By noticing where our attention automatically goes, we can step back and observe ourselves acting, feeling, or thinking in these habitual ways.

When we do this, we have accomplished a split of attention. We are engaged in acting, feeling, and thinking in real time. And a part of us is set apart, simply watching our small drama unfold, without judgment or design. This is a critical first step—to develop a dispassionate inner observer who can notice our unconscious ways of being. This has happened to most of us quite naturally at times, where we are actively "doing" life while a part of us observes us in that doing. Yet how do we cultivate that split of attention? How do we activate the inner observer to be present for us in everyday life?

A good practice to develop a proficient inner observer is meditation. Now, I don't necessarily mean sitting on a cushion for hours a day or going on a weekend retreat to find your observer. Meditation is nothing more than quieting oneself. It is often easier to notice the difference between the inner observer and our usual way of being by slowing down and closing our eyes for a moment. Quiet your mind, heart, gut by simply noticing your own breath. In and out, in and out, in and out.

Even when quiet, however, our minds are not silent. Thoughts, feelings, desires rise unbidden: How will I complete this project? I have to take the clothes out of the washer. I want a cup of tea. I'm bored. And so on. Allow them to arise and just let them go. Simply notice that they arise and leave. Now ask yourself who is noticing these thoughts, feelings, desires? The answer is your "inner observer."

Exercise: Activating the Inner Observer

Twice a day, set aside 15 minutes for activating the Inner Observer. Find a quiet space where you will not be interrupted. Turn off the phone if necessary. Sit quietly, close your eyes and just notice your breath as it enters and leaves your body. As thoughts, feelings, and other distractions come into your awareness, just note them and let them pass out of awareness. No judgement or holding on. Like leaves down a flowing stream, they come into view, pass through, and move on out of sight. Become aware of the part of you that is the Inner Observer, watching, without attachment. As you become more proficient at this noticing, you may find that the Inner Observer can help you at other times when you need clarity or distance from a situation you are engaged in.

Step Two: Paying Attention to Our Attention— the Nine Types

A basic precept from mystical tradition and modern sports psychology states that where attention goes, energy flows. The focus of our attention is very powerful. For instance, if we stub our toe, we fixate our attention on that painful, throbbing toe. It may even seem that all we are is *toe*. Nothing else is in our field of attention. Our focus is single-pointed for a time.

The focus of attention is similar for our Enneagram point. Our attention has an automatic place it goes, a default mode built into our personality. When we are not conscious of our default mode, our attention and energy are directed in habitual ways. We see only "what is right or wrong" (One) or "the worst-case scenario" (Six) or "other people's agendas" (Nine). All these attentional stances and others exist, yet we filter out those that don't fit our usual focus. We selectively see the same things all the time. In this way, the direction of our attention reinforces the personality's worldview. Yet attention can be trained. We can notice where it goes, and decide if we wish to override our default mode.

Each of the Enneagram points has a place where attention naturally migrates. Following is a list of our nine habitual ways of paying attention.

Perfectionist One

Attention naturally goes to noticing what is right or wrong, to perceiving error and correcting it, to continual improvement.

Giver Two

Attention naturally goes to what others need and how the Two can meet those needs to ensure the positive personal regard of others.

Performer Three

Attention naturally migrates to what will support an image of success, to gaining approval for one's accomplishments and image.

Romantic Four

Attention naturally migrates to what is missing in life. Others are felt to have what the Romantic is missing, inspiring intense longing.

Observer Five

Attention naturally goes to what others want from the Observer, and whether that will intrude upon or overwhelm his or her need for space.

Loyal Skeptic Six

Attention naturally turns to worst-case scenarios (envisioned in the mind) and the hidden motives of other people.

Optimist Seven

Attention naturally fixates on pleasant future plans and keeping all options open.

Straight Shooter Eight

Attention naturally goes to control—of people, personal space, and one's own vulnerability.

Mediator Nine

Attention naturally is focused on other people's agendas, and merging with them to the detriment of one's own agendas or desires.

Exercise: Observing Your Attention

Ask yourself at least three times a day "where is my attention now?" Set an alarm if you like or just ask yourself spontaneously. We are not only cultivating our inner observer now; we are training it to watch where our attention migrates. This is important for our third step: training our attention.

Step Three: Training Our Attention

With the aid of our inner observer we begin to notice when our attention fixates in the way peculiar to our own point. We then find we have a choice: Continue to focus attention in the usual fashion and act in our usual manner, or break the pattern by acting in a new manner or not at all. Our focus of attention has changed and behavior is no longer automatic. Even if we choose to act in a familiar pattern, it has become a choice rather than an unconscious, habitual response.

Exercise: Refocusing Your Attention

Notice an occurrence when your attention migrates to its habitual place—it will, even if your inner observer is extremely vigilant, so don't worry. Ask yourself if there is another vantage point from which to view this occurrence. Redirect your attention to this new view. Jot down or mentally note how your experience changes or remains the same. Note your thoughts, feelings, and sensations. Choose your action if one is called for. Notice if it is based on your habitual attentional stance, or if new information was added from your change of perception.

Step Four: Shifting Attention—Changing Viewpoints

We have the potential of all nine types within us. In childhood we chose one point as our way of perceiving, feeling, and acting in order to survive and get love in the world. As we learn more about the attentional stances of the other eight points, we can begin to shift or direct our attention to perceive as another Enneagram type might. Although we cannot change our core or default mode, we can see that we really only apply part of the range of human potential when our attention is directed in our habitual way. We empathize with others by shifting our attention in order to understand their worldview. More importantly, we expand our own perceptions at the same time.

Exercise: Shifting Your Attention

Engage in an ordinary activity that you do often—dishes, gardening, eating. Activate your inner observer and notice your thoughts, feelings, sensations as you are in the midst of it. Now choose an Enneagram point or worldview other than your own and engage in this same activity. How is this different? Similar? What thoughts, feelings, sensations are concomitant with your experience of this worldview?

Step Five: Be Gentle With Yourself

This is the most important step of all. In my years of teaching the Enneagram, I have been continually amazed at our capacity for compassion as we learn others' worldviews. I am equally amazed at our lack of compassion for ourselves. Often, as we embark upon our personal journey, we are focused on the destination. We want to be self-actualized, to reach our full potential as quickly as we can. Unfortunately, inner work cannot be rushed. It is a lifelong process to make our own acquaintance. There is no end point. The journey is the destination.

When we find ourselves repeating old patterns, acting or perceiving in ways that don't serve us, or simply going on automatic mode, we may berate ourselves. After all, we have the map—why aren't we getting there? Why is this still happening?

Our habitual mode and way of being *did* serve us well. It is just that we are ready to embrace more than our limited worldview. And as Tom Condon, author of *The Dynamic Enneagram*, is fond of saying, "Our Enneagram style developed from a place of complete sincerity." When we notice we have slipped into old habits, we can express gratitude for the role our personality has played in bringing us to this point.

Can we see the beauty, the perfection of our own worldview for just a moment? When a Five finds herself withdrawing again, it should not come as a big surprise. A Two finds himself denying his own needs. Of course it will happen again and again. We can learn to treat ourselves with as much compassion as if we were another person whom we are comforting. Remember, the Enneagram is a map of noticing and attention, not judgment.

Exercise: Gentleness Practice

Notice when you begin to judge yourself for not growing fast enough, for repeating old patterns, not learning from your mistakes, for just about anything. (Perfectionist Ones aren't the only people who judge themselves.) Stop and write your judgement down. Now imagine that a close friend or young person has come to you with the same story of judgement or self-criticism. What would be your advice to them? How would you counsel them? How would you soothe them and support their growth? Be as gentle with yourself as you would a child who needs your help and nurturing.

Step Six: Self-Disclosure

By telling our stories, sharing our growth and insights, and questioning others about their worldviews vis-à-vis their Enneagram type, we expand our knowledge and use of the Enneagram as a map of internal terrain. We often learn more about ourselves as we attempt to convey the experience of our internal terrain to others. To share a story or insight, to ask a question or promote discussion and inquiry among the worldwide Enneagram community, visit the *Gathering Place* bulletin board on the Essential Enneagram Web site at http://www.9points.com. You can dialogue with other Enneagram enthusiasts or ask a question of an Enneagram trainer. The bulletin board is monitored by an Enneagram teacher certified in the Oral Tradition™ with Helen Palmer.

Exercise: Sharing Your Worldview

Tell a little about your Enneagram worldview to a friend. No need to mention the Enneagram, just disclose a little of your own internal landscape. Open a dialogue with your friend. Was your disclosure a surprise to them? Old news? How did they see you? Often this will lead to an open discussion of one another's inner perceptions, thoughts, and feelings. Most of us are delighted that someone is interested in our internal terrain—it's just that no one ever asked!!

As you work with these steps, you'll notice that they seem so simple, even elementary. They are not easy, nor are they quick, yet they are essential to breaking free from the limitations of our Enneagram worldview. The path of self-development is best traveled with small, sacred steps.

Signposts—Danger Signals for All Nine Types

As we travel the journey of self-discovery using our Enneagram map, we find different obstacles for each of the nine types. How do we know when our personality is running us? If we are on autopilot, how do we make sure we notice it? A signpost would be helpful, sort of an alert on the map of potential obstacles ahead, a call to slow down so we can choose a response.

There are different signposts for each of the types. They show up on our personal journey as a thought or a feeling or a sense inside us. They are like a form of inner self-talk. The signposts serve as alerts for each of the types of personality in its default or automatic mode. As we learn the alerts most commonly associated to our Enneagram type, we can ask ourselves the following questions: As I notice these signposts along my personal journey, can I slow down and check the map? Can I then make the choice to continue along the same path consciously or perhaps choose another more suitable roadway—a detour around the automatic habit?

Perfectionist One

An alert that the personality is in automatic mode occurs when Perfectionist Ones find themselves feeling resentful or doing a slow burn. Key internal dialogue might include critical thoughts of others: No one else is pulling their weight. No one else can do it as well as I. If I don't do it, it won't get done, etc. Self-talk may also revolve around the inner critic run amok. Notice if you are continually comparing yourself with others—they are doing it better/worse than you.

While it is natural for the One to "sort" the environment by notic-ing what is wrong, there is a tendency to see a relationship, project, house, etc., as all wrong if a small part of it is flawed. The Perfectionist may want to scrap the whole project or relationship and begin again, rather than salvaging what is still "right." This philosophy of "throw-ing out the baby with the bath water" is a sure sign that the habitual mode of the personality is running things.

Giver Two

"No one appreciates me." "I just give and give, and for what?" Feeling unappreciated for all you've given or done is the main signpost for the Two. When it seems you are continually giving, but no gratitude is shown or no one is giving anything in return, you know the default mode is running.

When you find you are interested in a subject, hobby, or music you've never been interested in before, because someone you want to know better likes it, it is time to question whether you really want to pursue it. The Giver Two wonders, "Who should I be to guarantee your approval?" If you change your spots to match what you think another wants from you, you can be sure the habit is in full swing. Be wary if self-talk revolves around this person's "bringing out another side" of you.

Performer Three

When Threes find themselves wondering "How can I put the spin on this to make me (the project, the team) look good?" you know the automatic mode is running. Looking outward for how others are perceiving you and how to turn your endeavor into a success pulls the Performer away from asking themselves important questions: "Do I even want to do this project, be on this team, etc."

A tendency to "allow" others to think you have accomplished more than you have is a warning sign for Threes. When they find themselves adapting to their surroundings to appear successful to others or feel that they are playing a role, this signals that self-deceit is operating to convince the Performer they *are* their role or image.

Romantic Four

The feeling that something is missing from life is a signpost for the Four. Finding yourself focusing on the *one* person, detail, thing that would make this moment perfect is a clue that the Romantic personality is indeed operating in its automatic mode. It is possible to miss what is happening here and now when you are longing for what is missing.

Another sign that the personality is operating in its habitual way is when Fours find themselves feeling different from others or misunderstood. The focus on being unique and apart from results from the Romantic's worldview and is a portent that the habit is in control.

Observer Five

Detaching and dissociating from the circumstances around them— or wishing to withdraw—is the main signpost to alert Fives that their personality is on autopilot. Self-talk may include asking yourself how much others are going to want from you or wondering how you can give them what they want so you can leave.

Withholding information and hoarding knowledge serves as another alert for the Five that the habit is in control again. Minimizing their own needs can be another form of withholding and serves as a reminder to the Observer that the personality may be in the default mode again.

Loyal Skeptic Six

Whenever worst-case scenario "movies" begin playing for the Six, it is a call to notice that the doubting mind may be in control once more. The Loyal Skeptic's self-talk may include a series of "What if . . . happens?" and "What will I do if . . . happens?" When the what-ifs start spinning out, it is a sure sign that the habit is working to support the worldview.

When the Six notices everything is falling into place to substantiate a hypothesis, there's a good chance all evidence that would refute the hypothesis has been filtered from consciousness. Self-talk may reinforce the hypothesis by claiming "I knew it all along. I knew this would happen." This should alert the Loyal Skeptic to proceed carefully—it's a better than even chance that the personality is running its habitual gambit.

Optimist Seven

When the desire to experience something new, interesting, or exciting comes out of nowhere for the Seven, it is a clear signal that the personality is on automatic. Anxiety or difficult emotions can trigger the escape-into-experience mode for Sevens. Even an erudite escape into new knowledge is often the habit running the Optimist.

A tendency to miss the dark cloud for the focus on the silver lining signifies the Seven's automatic mode of reframing. It's almost alchemical—the Optimist converts painful, difficult situations into occasions for celebration. Self-talk often presents as "I know . . . happened, but what was good about it was . . . ." Loss is often converted to a new opportunity or challenge with no downtime for grieving. This giddy positivism is a sure sign that the personality is running the show.

Straight Shooter Eight

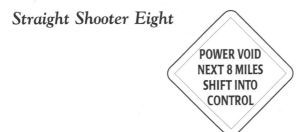

A sensing and compulsion to step into power voids where no one is taking control or making decisions (or even taking up energetic space) are hallmarks of the Straight Shooter Eight personality on autopilot. Self-talk may include "someone's got to do it or nothing will ever get done." "I don't want to be in control necessarily, but I don't want to be controlled."

The rising of feelings of vulnerability can set off Eight's habitual mode faster than anything else. These feelings are translated as boredom by the Straight Shooter and the classic antidote preferred is excess, whether it be in work, food, drink, partying, exercise, etc. Eights feel vital and invulnerable engaging their large energy so strongly. It's a sure bet that when excess is involved, the personality is really in control.

Mediator Nine

Procrastination is the default mode for the Nine. Difficulty with prioritizing often has the Nine putting off important tasks and issues in favor of nonessential substitutes. Self-talk often includes "Oh, I've got plenty of time, no problem." Another frequent internal phrase that pops up throughout the day is "I'll do that later." The Nine inevitably ends up feeling behind or pushed. These phrases should sound an alarm for Mediators that the personality is pushing them where they may not wish to go.

"It doesn't matter" is also common self-talk for a self-forgetter. "Whatever" is an easy way for Nines to get along with others, go with the flow, and allow the personality in its default mode to avoid the Mediator's true desires, preferences, and priorities.

All of these signposts are a *call to inaction*—to stop and get your bearings, to stop driving on autopilot and assess the next direction. We slow down and look within. Where am I? Where is my attention? Is this my automatic mode running me? What is the appropriate course? This is more difficult than it appears, because the habit of the personality is very strong. It had to be to ensure our survival and functioning in the world. We sure don't want to lose it or its gifts. We just don't want it to be the only game in town, robbing us of conscious, informed choice.

Perhaps there is a way to elicit the help of our personality in breaking its stranglehold on our emotions, thoughts, sensations, and perceptions. What if we were to engage the habitual mode of our Enneagram type to break the automatic pattern that runs us? Each of the nine types actually does have a unique way to trick our personality into helping us become more conscious of its default mode and our ability to choose our path.

Tricking the Fixation to Break
Its Hold on the Nine Types

Here are some simple (again, not easy) ways of getting your personality to work with you in your journey of self-development. Upon reflection, you may find others that work for you as well.

Perfectionist One: Frivolity as self-improvement

The Perfectionists' focus on improving themselves and becoming the best they can possibly be, often has them working even during their leisure time. Leisure pursuits include exercising, reading self-help literature, and taking classes that improve them. There is little time for frivolous, purely fun endeavors. We can engage the One personality to assist us by noting that frivolity and foolishness make one a better person. We learn about openness, spontaneity, and joy, which round us out as human beings.

Giver Two: Charity begins at home

Caring for others is how the Two ensures the lifeblood of connection. Sensing and meeting the needs of those important to the Giver is the automatic mode of the personality. Often, this externalization keeps the Two from knowing their own needs are not met, until they are completely drained and turn on those they care for.

This eruption can be disheartening and humiliating to the Giver. Eliciting the help of the personality, the Twos determine that giving to themselves and meeting their own needs are the best help they can offer to those significant to them. Then help flows from the Giver's full cup and doesn't drain them. Others feel no hook in their helping, no "giving to get," and a more genuine mutual relationship can develop.

Performer Three: "Being" increases my productivity

Multitasking Threes are generally in the midst of a whirlwind of activity. (I liken my husband at times to the Tasmanian Devil in the old Bugs Bunny cartoons.) Lots of balls are in the air at all times and continuous motion may become synonymous with accomplishment. Most Performers produce prodigiously, but they are not always efficient. Moving too fast can cause corners to be cut or jobs to need repair or extra work. The Three just keeps pushing through, continually doing.

In harnessing the personality, the Three Finds that *stopping* for periodic intervals actually can increase productivity by allowing contemplation of the best way to proceed. And, of course, these "being" breaks allow the Three to examine whether this endeavor is really an authentic desire or goal rather than the default of "I'll do it because I can make a success out of it."

Romantic Four: Finding the extraordinary in the ordinary

The Romantic's natural antipathy for all things ordinary or mundane can have the Four constantly searching for intense emotional experience. The high highs and low lows can be exhausting for the individual Four, as well as for those around them. Yet the Romantic believes that exhaustion and pain are small prices to pay for cultivating authenticity of experience. The habit can be tricked into breaking the automatic pattern when the Four decides that the most authentic of experience can be found in the ordinary, in the plain and simple things of life. The drive for authenticity can make this seeming flatness bearable until the Romantic truly discovers the extraordinary in the ordinary.

Observer Five: Language of the heart

The Observer's concern about having too little energy often leads them to withhold time and energy to be sure they have enough. This scarcity mode has the Five hoarding knowledge, time, even his presence. The fixated mode of the personality believes in the supremacy of mental knowledge. Yet the Five's lifelong quest for wisdom and understanding can be used to disrupt this habit of withholding when the Five begins to honor the wisdom and intelligence of the heart and emotions.

With the heart, the more energy you give, the more energy you have. It paradoxically seems to create more energy, the more you give it away to others. And as you share yourself and your knowledge with others, the more free they feel to naturally share their knowledge with you. It further relieves the Observer of expending energy in actively soliciting and grasping for knowledge.

Loyal Skeptic Six: Playing devil's advocate

The Six's tendency to take the opposite stance of the skeptic can be used to great advantage in disrupting the usual habitual mode of the personality. Loyal Skeptics can begin to question their own worldview by playing devil's advocate to what they believe to be true. The Six is hypervigilant to danger, downsides, and hidden motives. Yet Six can harness this vigilance in the service of scanning for upsides, positive visions, and the "good" in life. (I said it would be simple, not easy!)

When a Loyal Skeptic develops a hypothesis and begins looking for clues in the environment to support it, the opposite stance can be taken to look for clues that refute the Six's belief. Playing devil's advocate comes naturally to doubting Loyal Skeptics and can be invaluable in breaking the hold their fixation has on them.

Optimist Seven: Exploring the missing experience

Seven's gluttony for life experience causes the Optimist to wish to avail themselves of all life has to offer. "I don't want to miss anything," say most Sevens and herein lies the way to trick the personality into overcoming the default programming. Optimists avoid difficulty and the dark side of life—sadness, pain, limitation, etc. When Sevens believe they are missing half of life by turning away from this dark side, they are intrigued. If an interesting experience can be had by exploring this half of life, the Seven wants to find it. The desire to experience as much as possible of life can overcome the avoidance of difficulty and limits, helping the Seven along his journey of self-development.

Straight Shooter Eight: The invulnerability of vulnerability

The Straight Shooter is invested in being strong and believes that to be vulnerable is to be weak. But if the Eight considers the belief that only the strongest show their vulnerability, they may trick the personality enough to let them learn the truth that there is an inherent invulnerability in showing one's vulnerability. What more can they do to you? How can you be hurt, when you've already willingly shown the vulnerability that your enemies try to find? The control then is squarely in the Eight's hands, right where they want it.

An interesting twist to breaking the hold of the personality concerns the matter of control. Eights hate to be controlled, yet when the personality is operating in the habitual mode, that is exactly what is occurring. The Straight Shooter may break the pattern to reassert control—and to avoid being controlled by the default mechanism.

Mediator Nine: It's easier to do it now

Going with the flow can seem to ensure harmony and peacefulness for the Nine. The path of least resistance is the favorite of the Nine on automatic mode, and this ease in life can make it difficult for the Mediator to get things done in priority. "All things being equal" makes it hard to know the priority, and the innate faith of Nines that "things just work out for the best" can work against them. When a task or (even more difficult) authentic desire of the Nine comes into view on their screen, the internal turmoil that ensues—from conflicting things of equal weight—can have the Nine declaring inner peace by "not doing." It seems easier to get to it later.

"Later" is an amorphous sometime-in-the-future for the present-moment Nine. To harness the default mode of the personality, the Mediator must decide that it is genuinely easier to do it now and to finish it. The Nine must begin to believe that harmony will follow from engaging and completing, rather than waiting for a better time.

Personality as Helpmate

Activating the personality as helpmate in our personal development can be inordinately beneficial. We are able to use the considerable energy that keeps the habit in place, to our advantage. In essence, we are not actually tricking the fixation or automatic mode of the personality at all. We are uncovering a new truth while enlisting the habit's aid. We are opening ourselves to more than the limitations of our entrenched worldview.

To get the personality to collude with us and help us grow will be very simple using our "tricks," but it will not be easy. This may be some of the most difficult and rewarding work we have ever undertaken. To shift our inner beliefs and patterns will take observation of our inner landscape and asking "what if" questions, such as "What if it were true that frivolity would make me a better person?" "What if caring for myself first and filling my own cup really gives the greatest gift to my loved ones?" "How would I act differently?" "What small actions can I undertake to see if this is true for me?"

The Enneagram must be experienced and internalized to be truly useful as a map for our personal journey. Find what works for you. And don't forget to proceed with small, sacred steps.

Focusing on Our Gifts

We've established our starting point and plotted a course for our journey to know and develop ourselves. We know some of the obstacles of our Enneagram point and ways to break our habitual patterns. Yet our path would not be complete without a celebration and acknowledgment of our personality's gift. Often, we dismiss our gift quickly as we move on to the "real work" to be done, fixing, and toning our defective selves. I am continually amazed at my students (and myself!) when we forget we even have a gift already built into the default programming. Remember, default programming in a computer program or in our personality is there because it works when nothing else does, or when we can't figure out how to set our preferences or choices.

Revisiting our premise that where attention goes, energy flows, we find that a deliberate focus on our gifts helps them manifest more in our daily lives. We can add our inner observer to keep us honest, to help us notice and activate our gift, perpetuating a self-fulfilling prophecy.

Then the judgment of a One truly does become *discernment*. The Two's externalization to others' feelings turns to genuine *empathy*. The Three's frenetic multitasking becomes true *efficacy*. The Four moves from feeling different and special to offering an *authentic* unique contribution. Five's withdrawal becomes unattached clarity or *wisdom*. The Six moves from unconscious duty to loyal *commitment*. Seven's excessive giddiness turns to informed *optimism*. The Eight transforms excessive control to appropriate *strength*. The Nine transforms passive allowing to genuine *acceptance*. Our gifts are signposts we can notice, as well as obstacles. We are just less practiced at seeing our best. Acknowledging our strong points helps us integrate the best of our default mode with our new expanded ways of seeing, perceiving, and being. Our journey has just begun.

Exercise: Appreciating Your Gift

Take a few moments each day to reflect on your personality's gift. When were you last aware of it? How did it manifest? How might it show up in the future?

Figure 5-19 *Gifts of the Nine Types*

When we know ourselves better, when we understand the pitfalls and the gifts of our personality, when we are able to train our attention, then we are truly ready to meet another on his or her own ground. We are ready to honor someone else's reality. As we will explore in the next chapter, no place is this more challenging or rewarding than in our intimate relationships.

CHAPTER 6

The Enneagram and Relationships– Traveling Together Down a Path With Heart

*Relationships. We all got 'em, we all want 'em.
What do we do with 'em?*

—Jimmy Buffett

"I just don't understand why she (he) does that." "It seems like we have the same disagreements over and over." "Sometimes I believe men really are from Mars and women are from Venus!"

Even in the best relationships, there are instances when we are completely befuddled by our mate's actions or reactions. We simply have no construct, no map for understanding their "weird" behavior or what motivates them. Checking it out against our internal reality, we find no way in which it fits our worldview. It seems random, senseless, and strange to us. "Why are you doing this? Feeling this? Seeing this?"

The Enneagram guide can be at its most powerful when applied to our intimate relationships. True understanding begins when we can experience the worldview of others in our lives by *feeling* what reality feels like to them. By shifting our vantage point from our own particular version of reality to our intimate's internal perspective, we can find ways of dramatically improving our communication and connection.

Relating to another personality type is much like visiting another culture. The points on the Enneagram are like nine different countries, each with its own worldview, values, and belief system. In order to communicate with or visit one of these "countries," we need to learn a little about the language, customs, and cosmology. We must discover and enter the prevailing culture of each type. Only then can we begin to honor one another's unique differences, celebrate our human diversity, and enjoy "international" exchange.

Suppose you are to visit Thailand. You've never been there and you'd like to experience the culture. You begin by obtaining and studying a detailed map: a guidebook, which teaches you a little about the geography and beauty of the land. Maybe you will learn a little of the language and some of the customs and taboos. You discover you must never point your foot at a person or touch them on the head, since these gestures are considered rude and insulting in the extreme. As a visitor to the culture, you want to be sure to honor the Thai people.

Yet even if you were to read every Thailand guidebook in existence, you would still know only a very little bit about any individual Thai person. The rest of your experience of this unfamiliar culture would best be served by attentive exploration with an open heart and mind.

If we approach our intimate relationships as a journey to a new culture that has much to offer and teach us, we truly find a path with heart. The Enneagram in this chapter will be expanded to a travel guide to assist us in our mutual exploration.

Let us start our guidebook with some generic "traveler's hints" to prepare our minds and hearts for open exploration. These hints may help us leave behind the cultural bias of our own Enneagram type long enough to truly appreciate another worldview. We've learned through the work in self-development with the inner observer how to recognize and stand back from our automatic mode. This creates an open space in our internal landscape where learning and appreciating another culture can take place. *Our first step is to let go of what we know.*

Traveler's Hint #One:
There Is No Such Thing as "Objective Reality"

Each of us is so used to living in our own culture, our own personality, we have come to believe this is reality. All nine worldviews are equally entrenched in believing they know the truth of objective reality. A Loyal Skeptic Six "knows" the world is an inherently dangerous place, and that vigilance and plans are your best chance of attaining security. A Mediator Nine "knows" good things come to those who wait—most things work out for the best anyway, so why worry and rush around when it feels so much better to be peaceful? A Straight Shooter Eight "knows" only the strong survive in this jungle we call life and that the truth will out in a good fight. A Romantic Four "knows" authenticity is only to be found in deep feeling and intense emotional connection. Reality is colored and created by our perceptual bias. In fact, we actually sort information to support our worldview, ignoring or filtering out contradictory evidence.

Dick, a Six, worries when he and his One wife, Belinda, fight. As a Loyal Skeptic, he moves directly to the worst-case scenario: They are getting divorced. He feels devastated and begins planning to get a place and move out, etc. Belinda is shocked when he finally voices this. She says from her Perfectionist perspective, a fight is just that: healthy conflict to work out a problem. She admits she doesn't let go of their fights right away, but simmers and withdraws for a while. According to her, she needs time to work through her post-disagreement resentment. However, Dick reads her silence as "she wants out, doesn't love me or want to be married to me anymore."

The Enneagram has illuminated their default modes for them, as well as their partner's perspective. They have agreed to disagree. Dick now gives Belinda time to work out her anger (although it still activates his doubt). Belinda tries to remember to reassure him that a disagreement is not a crisis in their relationship.

When stressed or angry, it can be difficult to remember your loved one has a separate-but-equal objective reality. For this reason, it is important that we continue the work we began in self-development of stepping back from our own default mode and questioning our own perspective. We attribute feelings and thoughts to our loved one based on the cues we observe from them. Yet these cues are nearly always filtered through our habitual personality or worldview. As we work with our partner in a relationship, we can enlist their aid in corroborating or correcting the assumptions of our worldview. We can notice how often we are off the mark, and begin a process of inquiry to learn our partner's objective reality.

Traveler's Hint #Two:
When in Rome, Do as the Romans Do

Honor the culture you are entering. Learn enough of the customs, language, and energetics of emotional intelligence for the land you are visiting. This is easier than we initially think. Remember that we all had the potential of all nine types in us at the beginning, so shifting our worldview takes paying attention and being fully present. At some level, it is not a completely unknown territory. We can learn by immersing ourselves in another culture, another worldview. We will only be richer for it.

My friend Bronwyn Cooke was on assignment for *National Geographic* photographing a group of women who live high in the Himalayan peaks in Hunza, Pakistan. Bronwyn spoke not a word of their language, nor did these women speak any English. Very little information was available about their culture, customs, etc. (That's why the *Geographic* sent Bronwyn there.) Bronwyn wondered anxiously how she would communicate, much less take any photographs. Then she forgot what she knew and responded in the moment.

She saw a woman come out of a hut, pour water into a bowl, and begin to carefully wash up. Bronwyn went over to the woman and gazed at her when the woman locked eyes with her and smiled. Quite naturally, Bronwyn simply began to bathe with her. They smiled and shared a common experience. When Bronwyn finally raised her camera as the woman was braiding her hair, she smiled her consent to the photographs. Through openness and a willingness to explore, following the lead of the cultural expert, Bronwyn had no trouble communicating and building a relationship.

Meeting our intimate where he or she lives involves momentarily letting go of what we "know" and exploring the world they inhabit. We can immerse ourselves in the culture of our loved one by entering their worldview and experiencing it from within.

Traveler's Hint #Three:
Leave Your Own Country Behind

Travel lightly. Your own baggage will only cloud things, so leave behind as much of it as you can. If you do take your own history and worldview into a communication of cultures, do so from a learning perspective, as an invitation to open inquiry. "I see it like . . . . How is this for you?" "Is this a Three thing?" "A Nine thing?" "It looks like X is happening, is that true?" "What is your experience of this?" We can communicate with an unfamiliar culture by exercising openness and presence, and leaving behind for a moment our Enneagram "country" or culture.

Cultural misunderstandings can occur from seemingly small gestures or communications (such as rudely pointing your toes at a Thai person). Similarly, when different Enneagram cultures meet in intimate relationships, it often seems that little things can make or break the relationship. Pandemonium can surface from tiny details of everyday life, if we only view reality from our own perspective and miss the view from our intimate's perspective. Scores of little misunderstandings result in cultural conflict and standoffs. We often act like the stereotypical "ugly American" visiting another culture, believing that repeating our viewpoint or speaking our language more loudly will make us understood. Little squabbles can expand into major difficulties in relationships. Our best bet is to drop our automatic reference point and open to that of our intimate's. We can enlist our partner's help in learning and seeing reality from their view, and a mutual expansion of reality can result. Let me illustrate with two "little things" from my relationship.

I am a Seven and my husband is a Three. It is important to him to present the right image, especially in his work, speaking to corporations. Often he will come to me bearing three wonderful ties, all of which match his current outfit. "Which one should I wear?" he asks. From my own Optimist viewpoint, they all look good so it doesn't matter. Yet if I were to answer accordingly, it would completely dishonor his Performer viewpoint. I try to see from inside the Three for a moment—and tie selection seems critically important from that perspective.

He is having an image crisis; this tie selection is a survival issue. In order to truly honor him, I must realize this, take a deep breath, and really turn my complete attention to choosing one. And surprisingly, I find it takes no more time to honor his viewpoint than to substantiate mine. (Notice that I turned my attention to choosing the tie—we are back to noticing and directing attention as we did in our self-development work.)

I, on the other hand, am driven by fear. (Remember Sevens are the fear type who forgot they were afraid.) We were driving in a torrential downpour one late Florida night. My goal-directed Performer spouse was passing all the obstacles on the highway, determined to reach our airport destination. The other cars were simply in the way. I succumbed to fear, seeing crumpled steel and our broken bodies in my imagination. Finally I could stand it no longer. "Could you slow down a little?" I asked shakily.

Dewitt looked over at me and in a rapid shift to my Optimist perspective declared, "Oh my God, you're scared, aren't you?" I nodded as he took his foot off the gas and coasted in behind a truck in the slow lane. "It would never occur to me to be scared; I feel in complete control of the situation. Still, it is never my intention to frighten you. I simply don't operate from fear. I only want to get there. But hey, we aren't really late, and it doesn't matter that much to me." Before knowing the Enneagram and the difference in our "cultures," Dewitt felt he might have just said "Oh, that's stupid. There's nothing to be afraid of, I'm in complete control. Don't worry," and just kept passing the obstacles. It would have been the perfect set-up for a major blow-up—all from a tiny misunderstanding of worldviews.

Traveler's Hint #Four:
Take Time to Know a Culture Deeply

One assumption we might make is that we know our intimates or loved ones very well already. After all, we have been visiting the person who inhabits this Enneagram point for some time already. Yet like learning about a place, discovering the inner culture and worldview of our intimate takes time and attention. When we use our Enneagram guidebook as a place to begin inquiry with a common language, we find previously unexplored territory in ourselves as well as our mates. This need not be cause for dismay that we did not know our loved one as well as we thought we did. Rather, it is an opportunity for deepening our relationship, for going farther together down the path with heart than we ever thought possible.

Jennine, a Five, confided, "Before I knew the Enneagram, I was wondering if there was something wrong with my husband, Daniel. He seemed so clingy asking for reassurance that I loved him when I just wanted to be alone or think. I'd want to go running—alone—and he'd constantly want to come with me. When I found out he was a Loyal Skeptic Six and might perceive my very strong needs for privacy as abandonment, or at the very least, cause for doubting the relationship, I became more understanding. He's also been learning about my Observer Fiveness and giving me more private space."

Daniel shares, "I'm even finding that when she goes off on retreat or to an art class for a week alone—I am making plans for my own trips. I renew old acquaintances or see places I've wanted to revisit. I really have begun to enjoy it. And I'm becoming more comfortable with my own doubt—and now know it has much more to do with me than with Jennine."

Traveler's Hint #Five: Get a Local Guide

When we visit a new culture or country, it can be invaluable to have a native guide to show us around and acquaint us with the local customs, mores, and worldview. In relationship, our partner is the true expert in his or her own internal terrain. The Enneagram can give us a general glimpse when we know our intimate's type, but the subtleties will be best learned from our local guide: our partner in the relationship journey.

Les, an Straight Shooter Eight, is a Marine colonel in a high-level position. His wife, Maria, is a Six. They've been married for more than twenty years and have a very solid relationship. Yet Les claims the Enneagram has given him new ways of honoring his wife, now that he knows more of her Loyal Skeptic internal terrain.

For example, the commanding general was expected for dinner with several dignitaries. Les brought home the groceries and dropped the milk, which burst and spilled in the front hall. "Now I know what she went through internally when I dropped the milk: 'The meal will be ruined, the evening will be a disaster, the general will be furious and fire you, we'll be out on the street cold and hungry.' And all this will take place in a nanosecond.

"Now knowing the movies that spontaneously play in her head, I reassure her, let her know I understand her concern, and give her a reality check on the likelihood that this scenario will actually occur—and I rush out to get more milk ASAP! I never tell her 'don't worry.' That would be like telling the sun not to shine. Likewise she doesn't tell me to 'calm down.'"

Another couple who benefitted from sharing worldviews are Matt and Debbie. Matt is a Perfectionist One initially drawn to his Optimist Seven wife Debbie by her positive outlook and adventurous spirit. Nineteen years later, with a lovely home and family, Debbie found Matt too rigid and controlling at times—too serious. Matt still found Debbie fun, but often felt she was flighty and dilettantish. When she reframed his concerns and problems, he felt misunderstood.

The Enneagram map began a journey of change for them, individually and together in their relationship. Matt began to realize that his default mode of taking on excess responsibility and "forgetting" to allow himself pleasure was actually having adverse effects. During the little time off from work he did have, he was usually angry and resentful. This hurt his relationship with his wife and family. When he learned that taking time for his own pleasure was actually meeting more of his family's needs than working longer hours, he began to take extra time off on a regular basis. The Enneagram helped Matt "lighten up"—mostly on himself.

Debbie began to slow down and feel her pain and hurt from childhood. In confronting old difficulties, she found herself able to focus more clearly. She began a course of intensive study in the Enneagram itself and it has grown into a career and business for her.

Most importantly, Matt and Debbie find themselves in a relationship with very different people. Both have grown and changed extensively. While it wasn't easy, their inner journey together worked because both of them were committed to their own growth as well as that of the relationship. They integrated the Enneagram map into their travels of self- and mutual discovery and claim they are more deeply in love now than ever before.

Exercise: Building Cultural Understanding

We can begin to build connection and compassion by understanding our different viewpoints. Here's an exercise for partners to begin this exploration of one another's internal terrain. On a sheet of paper, write your answers to the following questions from your own perspective. Have your partner do the same from his or her perspective. Do not share your answers with one another yet.

1. What is most important in a relationship is _____

_____

2. What I look for in a partner is_____

_____

3. Life is really about _____

_____

4. One way my partner can honor who I am is_____

_____

5. One way I can honor my partner is_____

_____

On a separate sheet of paper, answer these same questions from your partner's or significant other's perspective. In other words, if you began to look out from your intimate's eyes and inhabit his or her worldview, how would you answer the following questions. Have your mate answer the same questions as if he or she were answering from your worldview.

Now sit down together and share your answers with one another. No matter what the results, you'll find you've begun the process of inquiry and exploration that leads to greater intimacy. Relationship is a commitment to exploration—a shared journey of knowing ourselves. As we learn the internal landscape of our loved one, we find it comes naturally to honor their "culture."

As we become more skilled in using the Enneagram map as a guide in relationships, we begin to internalize it, to make it our own. This guide, like any other, is only a starting point. The Enneagram gives us tools and a framework for beginning the work of exploring the internal landscape of ourselves and the significant others in our lives.

Initially we must understand our own worldview, so we can effectively get it out of the way long enough to experience the worldview of our spouse, partner, or friend. We may use the common language of the Enneagram to help communicate our growth and changes to one another. Since we don't stay the same, we will be continually exploring our internal landscape as well as that of our partner. Ultimately, we may be able to "lose" the map and simply experience the complexities and nuances of our partner's unique worldview. After all, the map is a poor substitute for the richness of the actual territory. Besides, we can always come back to it if we lose our way.

Enneagram Matches—Finding a Mate

I often hear "What Enneagram personality type is best for me to be with? What type goes best with a One?" I've seen all the combinations of type work together. I've seen the same combinations become total disaster. We can't match people by personality type, anymore than we can state that certain personality types will be drawn to particular cultures or countries. I'm drawn to Bali and the American Southwest. Another Seven might feel closest to the forests of Canada or the moors of England. We look for a resonance and we look for qualities important to us.

In my search for a mate, I realized I was looking for a man who was sensitive, not afraid to share feelings, on a spiritual path, and more committed to truth than comfort. What Enneagram type would match that? Luckily, I didn't use the Enneagram to even narrow my search and found all these qualities—in a Three! Had I been looking for a specific Enneagram type to embody these virtues, a Three would prob-ably have been last on my list.

Yet who can blame us for wanting to make sense of relationships and finding a mate? We want an answer: Who should I be with? Who am I sympatico with? How can I find someone to accompany me on that path with heart? Although we know deep inside there is no easy answer, we keep hoping to narrow the field when we are searching for someone to share our life.

> Vanessa, a Three, is a good friend of ours. She felt that Dewitt and I had the ideal relationship. Although she knew better (She is an Enneagram teacher!), she decided to look for a Seven to share her life, hoping to duplicate our Seven-Three combination. Despite initial attraction and seeming compat-ibility, the relationship was filled with turmoil and difficulty. It ended with bad feelings on both sides. "I got hammered," says Vanessa morosely. "I know I'm not supposed to find a type. I just thought that maybe . . . ."

We cannot choose a mate on the basis of their Enneagram type. Human beings are much too complex for that. We *can* look for quali-ties that are important to us. We *can* choose a partner willing to undertake the journey of self-exploration and commitment to learning and sharing together. And we *can* choose to honor the culture and reality of the fellow traveler who becomes our mate.

When Enchantment With the New Gets Old

My spouse and I visited Molokai, Hawaii, many years ago. It was love at first touch of our feet upon the land. Delighting in the laid-back rural lifestyle, we were thrilled at the limited range of choice—and how out-of-touch Molokai seemed with the busy-ness of the mainland and even the other Hawaiian islands. This is our true home, we de-cided. Our first love. The land grabbed hold of us and made us her own. Like new lovers, we proclaimed her charms daily: The people are so friendly and caring! The land is so beautiful! Primarily agricultural Molokai is old Hawaii at its best. Our new love was idealized: There is no crime on Molokai. Molokai is low stress and back-to-nature values.

When we moved into our home for six-plus months each year, we were still in the honeymoon phase. We imposed an idealization of our own worldviews onto Molokai: a limited understanding of a complex culture. Now, years later, we have come to know her better. The land remains beautiful, but there are serious questions about her development and economy. The "Friendly Isle" has to deal with growth issues. Stress is inevitable where unemployment is high and options are few. We don't love her less, but we love more of her culture as viewed from the inside and we are still learning. We are developing a more intimate relationship with our home.

A new relationship is like visiting a country or culture for the first time. Everything is charming in its newness and its difference. Yet living in this new culture day-to-day may cause you to find irritating some of the very things that charmed and delighted you in the beginning. The culture has not changed, our intimate has not changed, but our perception has shifted. For a brief time, we may have suspended our worldview in favor of another. Even more likely, we simply idealized all we saw. As the mist of newness clears from our eyes, we begin to find fault, using our worldview as a reality measuring stick. Let me give a couple of examples.

Patty, a Giver Two, fell in love with Mark, a Mediator Nine. For the first couple of years, she extolled his many virtues: how easygoing he was, how much he seemed to enjoy life, how talented he was, yet surprisingly not driven or workaholic. Then her tune began to change and she complained about his lack of a preference about where they lived, where they vacationed, or even where they went out to dinner. She was angry that he was "wasting" his considerable talent, when he could "do so much more."

It took some time—and the Enneagram—for Patty to realize what had initially attracted her to Mark, was now becoming the source of discord. Mark hadn't changed, yet her reaction to his attributes had, once the idealization had worn off. Patty found herself working to support Mark in his own development, while rediscovering the gifts she loved in him. She began to honor Mark's worldview, while they both strove to break out of their habitual modes: his tendency to submerge his own desires and priorities, and hers to help change him into her vision of his full potential. Together they are building a stronger, deeper relationship.

Disenchantment in the Nine Types

As attraction gives way to friction in relationships, it will be help-ful to consider how each of the nine types comes to be viewed. To better detect the worldview in its automatic or habitual mode, here are the nine worldviews in brief, and ways the mate often may automati-cally perceive each of the types once the newness of relationship has worn off. These descriptions can act as a quick reference that one or both of you may be operating in the default mode of the personality.

Perfectionist One

Worldview: Attention automatically goes to what is right or wrong in a situation (or in a partner), to what needs improving. Life is about con-tinuing to improve toward a set of high internal standards.

A One's mate may initially love the high moral and ethical ground, sense of responsibility, dependability, high level of discernment, etc. Later the mate may find the Perfectionist nitpicky, judgmental, and critical—never satisfied. They may feel the One is not fun anymore; there's always more to be done first. The One now seems to be trying to control them when offering suggestions for personal improvement.

Giver Two

Worldview: Attention automatically goes to helping others, to sensing and giving others what they need, to being indispensable, to feeling others' feelings so strongly they may not know their own.

Initially the mate may love the giving, loving empathy of the Two. The strong emotional connection is very attractive, as is being the center of the Giver's attention. Later the mate may find there are strings at-tached to the Two's giving. Something is expected and they have no clue as to what it is. "If you loved me, you'd know," says the Giver. (Because Twos themselves don't know what they want!) Besides, the Giver's mate may not need or want what is given. "Why are you trying to fix me? I'm not broken," the mate asserts. Being the center may become intrusive rather than desirable.

Performer Three

Worldview: Attention habitually goes to doing—to achieving and ap-pearing successful. Threes can adjust their behavior to present the image that is wanted. And they can identify with that image so strongly, their true self is not known.

Initially the Performer's mate may love the dedication to work, even the successful image. Later they may resent the always-doing, always-networking workaholic mode. There may be less time for relationship. "We used to spend time together, now I hardly ever see him (her)," decries the mate of a Three. Brusqueness from the normally charming Three may shock his or her mate, should they get between the Performer and the accomplishment of their goals.

Romantic Four

Worldview: Attention automatically goes to what is missing in life. "Something distant or unattainable will make me complete." "What is here in front of me isn't quite it." "If only I had . . . " "If only I were . . . " To the Four, deep emotions are the only authentic truth in life. They experience ordinary everyday life as flat.

A mate may be drawn to the depth and feeling of the Romantic, to their uniqueness and sensitivity. Later they may discover the Four rejects them when they get too close, then again desires and woos them when they pull back. Also their mate may have difficulty with Four's intensity and emotionality—it can be too much, like playing the same record too often.

Observer Five

Worldview: Attention habitually goes to protection of privacy and personal space. "What do people want from me?" "How much am I going to be required to put out?" Protecting their strong need for privacy and distance, Fives prefer to take an observing role at parties or in groups. Observers think about things carefully, including feelings.

The Five's mate is often drawn to their self-sufficiency and ability to remain detached in the face of chaos. While they initially appreciate the Observer's exceptional ability to think things through, later they may feel rejected by their intimate's need for privacy and alone time. An Observer's mate can feel hurt by a Five's detachment and failure to access and discuss feelings.

Loyal Skeptic Six

Worldview: Attention automatically goes to what is threatening or dangerous in the world. This is the planner who allows for worst-case scenarios so they won't be surprised. The Loyal Skeptic can either flee or be openly confrontational in the face of what is feared or dangerous.

A Six's mate is drawn to their loyalty and careful planning. In the beginning, they are fascinated by the Loyal Skeptic's imagination. But later the Six's mate may be hurt when the attention to worst-case scenario extends to their relationship. When the Six looks for clues that there is something wrong with the relationship ("I know you're going to leave me."), often ignoring evidence to the contrary, the Loyal Skeptic's constant worry and negativism may be difficult for their mate.

Optimist Seven

Worldview: Attention habitually goes to pleasurable alternatives, enjoyable future plans. Numerous options are kept open at all times. The Optimist may have difficulty committing to one person, needing to keep many possibilities open. Thus, the fun-loving Seven avoids pain and emotional discomfort.

A mate is initially drawn to Seven's zest for life and adventure as well as their childlike ability to have fun. But that can wear thin when the Optimist won't acknowledge difficulties or pain. Serious discourse about problems is out of the question for this eternal escapist who frustrates their mate in any attempt to work on problems in the relationship. When the going gets tough, the Seven is outta there and their inability to truly commit may be difficult for their mate.

Straight Shooter Eight

Worldview: Attention goes to being strong: strength is the key to survival in the world, to taking command and control. Lust for life and excess prove Eight's own invulnerability to himself. "What you see is what you get," says the direct Straight Shooter.

The Eight's mate may feel protected and safe with the Straight Shooter's strength. At first, they may be drawn to the energy and vitality of Eight's no-holds-barred approach to life. But the controlling can be hard to live with after a time, when one starts to feel bullied. The Straight Shooter's impatience with emotion and their inability to show vulnerability can be hard for their partner. And at times, an Eight's directness in social situations can embarrass their mate.

Mediator Nine

Worldview: A Nine's attention automatically migrates to other people's preferences while forgetting his or her own. Mediators keep the peace that way. These mellow laid back acceptors of the Enneagram can see all points of view equally, making it hard to choose a specific course of action or know their own desires.

Initially a Nine's mate may feel totally accepted and loved just for who they is. Feeling calmer around the Mediator's peacefulness, they admire this faithful approach to life. Later on they may become irritated if Nine doesn't make decisions easily, if they just seem to float through life. The mate may feel they can't count on their Mediator partner because they don't take life seriously enough. In the end, their partner mate may become impatient or angry when the Nine is unable to state a preference, if they say "whatever you like."

Exercise: Exploring Disenchantment

Quickly and privately, write the answers to the following questions on a sheet of paper, while your spouse or partner does the same.

What first attracted me to my friend/partner was: _____

_____

What bothers me sometimes is _____

_____

What has changed? My viewpoint or my partner? How? (Answer as honestly as you can.) _____

_____

_____

What still delights me about my partner is_____

_____

_____

Share your answers with one another. Use this exercise as an inquiry into your own motivations and Enneagram bias. See if you can assist one another in seeing the filters of the habitual mode. It will be good practice for later, when you can be an observer for one another, when the habit seems to be in control and the inner observer is asleep.

Changes in Perspective

When the very same qualities that we valued in the beginning of a relationship develop into annoyances and conflict later on, we'd like to say our *partner* changed. But what is more likely is that our perceptions have changed. In other words, we begin to see the downside of the gift of each of the types.

At first, we idealized our partner's attributes. We were enchanted by the newness and otherness in front of us. Then as the enchantment wore off, we began to return to our own automatic worldview and to measure our partner by our own reality. Of course, since our partner is not the same as we are, they will be found wanting if we believe the world is truly the way we view it.

The Enneagram shows us there are very different perceptions of reality from our own worldview that are just as valid. Our personal worldview can be constricting when we are bound by it, when we are unable to pull back to observe it or adjust our attention in other ways. When we learn to suspend our automatic reality, to see through the eyes of another—if only for a moment—we open to the truth of other worldviews. And thus, we expand our capacity for understanding and perceiving.

Naturally we won't be able to sustain suspension of our worldview for any length of time; we will always return to our personality. Yet we will learn in momentarily shifting worldviews to honor our intimates, that all nine views have an inherent beauty, and each type's perspective has its own perfection. There is no one viewpoint that is better than another—they are simply different. As Helen Palmer says, "Each type has one-ninth of the truth." When we viscerally understand this, compassion blooms without effort. We begin to expand our vision—to see the world from our loved one's stance, enough to honor their culture wholeheartedly.

New levels of intimacy are possible using the Enneagram as a guide. A common language now exists for expressing feelings, motivations, inner life. We have the questions to deepen our inquiry into our intimate's inner landscape. Even if we should spend years in this or any new culture, we won't know all there is to know about it: We'll discover deeper and deeper levels of meaning. As we deepen the journey of connection with our loved ones, we find that we will never completely know the mystery of this beloved human being. A new and more profound exploration is possible when we synergize our points of view in the service of our relationship journey.

Exercise: Relating Through the Centers

This exercise in relating is done with your intimate, partner, or friend. Allow at least thirty minutes to complete it and debrief.

Choose one person to be the receiver, to notice the energy. The other will be the sender. Set a timer (an egg timer is ideal) for three minutes. The sender will talk about an everyday occurrence (e.g., describing the drive to the office) or any subject that has little emotional weight or charge. It can be your grocery list . (Please do not read anything, though. This is a monologue.)

For the first three minutes, the sender will focus attention on his own head center while speaking. The receiver will not speak, just notice the energy of the sender. When the first three minutes are up, flip over or reset the timer. The sender continues speaking, this time focusing attention on his heart center. Repeat with three minutes of the sender focusing attention on the gut center. The receiver does not speak, just notices energy from the sender.

Now repeat the exercise switching roles: the sender becomes the receiver, while the receiver becomes the sender. Upon completion of the exercise, discuss with one another any feelings, sensations, thoughts, etc., that came up. Was there a difference in the quality of relating from the different centers? Describe it. Is there a center you feel you utilize more than others when relating?

What we learn from this exercise is that an entire interaction may be dramatically changed by the center we inhabit while communicating. The content may not change at all, but the energy conveys very different messages than do mere words. We are sensitive to this and respond more to the energy than to the literal message.

Most of us have had the experience of receiving a heart-to-heart talk from another that just plain didn't work. The sender may have been having a heartfelt discussion from his or her head, which conveys detachment, disconnection, even fear. The words are right, but the feeling is wrong, creating dissatisfaction for both sender and receiver. Perhaps the sender was coming from the gut in this sensitive discussion, causing the receiver to tune into strength, control, action, even anger. Both parties end up feeling misunderstood and unfulfilled. Yet use the exact same words from the heart center, and we intuitively sense affinity and feeling behind them. It truly becomes a *heart-to-heart* talk. We are no longer reacting to control or detachment but responding to connection. The quality of the discussion is completely changed.

The heart center is not the only one we'll need to access in communicating with our intimates. We may need to appropriately set some boundaries and focus our attention on the strength of our gut center. If we want to create a future plan with our partner, we'll want to access the visionary qualities of the head center.

The important thing is to become conscious of which energy center our attention is focused in. Are we focused within our head, our heart, or our gut? Is that the appropriate center for this interaction? Which one is? This doesn't have to be a secret. If your partner is working on this with you, discuss the type of interaction you are experiencing. What centers should both of you focus on? What would best serve the goal of the discussion and the relationship itself?

Practice noticing your own and your intimate's activated energy centers when discussing daily minutiae, things with no emotional charge. As you become proficient at communicating with and from each center in a relaxed state, it will be easier to do so when a difficult discussion or argument occurs.

A number of books that explore how the various combinations of the nine types play out together in intimate relationship—Helen Palmer's *The Enneagram in Love and Work* and Baron and Wagele's *Are You My Type? Am I Yours?* are two I highly recommend. Because this ground has been covered so thoroughly and well, I won't reiterate these combinations here. Instead, I'd like to focus on an area where I see much more discord and difficulty in intimate relationship: subtypes.

Subtypes—the Subcultures of the Enneagram

As if it weren't difficult enough learning to get along in a new culture, we also have to learn subcultures. In our guidebook about Thailand, there may be nuances to the general culture, additive factors, cultures within the culture. For example, the seaside folk may live differently from the mountain folk. The urban cosmology may be markedly different from the rural, even though they share the same general view of the world. These subcultures further define areas where misunderstanding or conflict can occur from a clash of worldviews.

The Enneagram has subcultures as well. In addition to the nine types, there are three main "subtypes" or "instinctual types" that offer a whole new level of challenge to intimate relationships. To be sure, many of the couples I see in workshops or in consultation have more significant worldview clashes related to differences in their subtypes than to differences in their basic Enneagram types.

Each Enneagram type is further divided into three instinctual types or subtypes. These subtypes reflect the basic human instincts of *self-preservation, social standing* in relation to the herd or group, and the drive for *one-to-one relating* (also referred to as sexual subtype or sexual instinct by some Enneagram authors.) Each of us has all three instincts programmed into us. The Enneagram subtype is the main instinctual arena (or arenas) where the underlying drive is channeled or played out.

The underlying drive for each type (lust for the Eight, Sloth for the Nine, Anger for the One, Fear for the Six, etc.) might be likened to a current of energy. This current branches off into three separate areas that represent the instincts of self-preservation, social standing, and one-to-one relating. The strength of each instinct, that is where attention habitually goes, will determine the amount of flow down each branch of current (see Figure 6-1). It is completely individual and varies person to person. Often one instinct or branch is very large, with less flow down the other two. Occasionally there are two large flows, with a mere trickle flowing down the third. Rarely, an individual is automatically balanced among all three.

For example, I have habitually focused very strongly on the one-to-one relating instinct. Much of my attention has centered on my intimate relationship. I have concentrated some energy on self-preservation: I never travel without my own coffee and portable coffeemaker. However, I generally spent very little attention on my social standing within a group; I was essentially uninterested in groups. So my current of attention would have had a large flow down the one-to-one branch, a moderate flow down the self-preservation branch, and a trickle down the social branch.

Ideally, we would like to have three fairly balanced branches attending equally to our natural human instincts. Yet when we are unconscious of them, we are often driven by one to the detriment of the others.

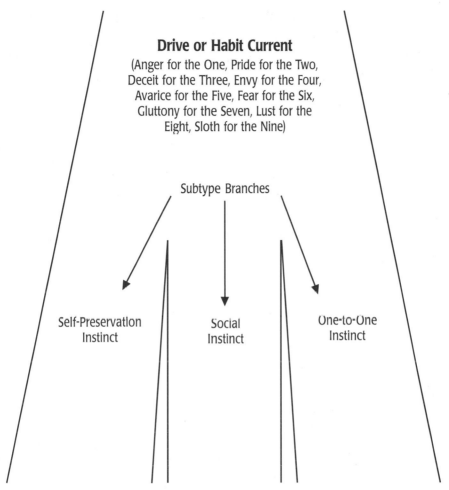

Figure 6-1 *Where attention goes, energy flows.*

Exercise: Discovering Your Subtype

Reflect where your attention seems to be directed. Are you most concerned with survival issues—food, shelter, safety, family and self-preservation issues?

Are you most concerned with social issues? With attention to group activities? (It may not necessarily be that you are drawn to be *in* a group—some social subtypes have strong antipathies against being part of a group. However, their attention is still drawn to groups.) They can focus on several people at a time—people with a common cause or who share common interests.

Are you most concerned with one-to-one relating? Do you prefer to relate to only your significant other or a small number of very close friends? Do you feel like going deeply into conversation with one person when in a group or at a party?

Often we have blind spots regarding which instinct our attention is most concentrated on. Ask your spouse or partner where he or she feels you focus your attention most often.

Instinctual types or subtypes aren't only another venue where differences show up between intimates; similarities also affect our relating. All self-preservation subtypes—those most concerned with survival and safety issues—share a particular similarity of worldview. Although an Eight and a One have very different essential worldviews, if both are focused on self-preservation, they'll have a meeting of the minds regarding what is important in life. We can see potential friction between the worldviews of a One and a Seven, yet if both direct the majority of their attention to social issues or functioning within a group (community, social cause, church, even a group of friends, etc.), they find a common worldview within the context of their separate positions.

Matt and Debbie have been married nineteen years. In that time, they have had their share of disagreements based on the collision of the paradigms of One and Seven. However, one mainstay of their relationship has centered around a place where they share a view of the world. They are both self-preservation subtypes concerned with safety and security. Consequently, they channel the majority of their attention and energy into the self-preservation instinct.

They have two large refrigerator-freezers stuffed with food, "just in case." Also they were in complete accord that their home needed an alarm system and that they would stock up on extra wood each fall on the chance it might be an unusually cold winter.

When Dewitt and I, who are both one-to-one subtypes, told them we had gotten rid of our car phone after only two months, they were appalled. We had found it a pain to deal with while driving and found we didn't really want to use it. Simultaneously, they burst out, "But you need it for your safety. What if the car breaks down?" We looked at them blankly. We had never considered that use very seriously. Since all four of us drive late model cars, Dewitt asked, "When was the last time any of us broke down?" We had each had a flat tire or other mishap once in the last seven years. But that was not important. As Matt and Debbie pointed out, "You never know where you'll be the next time, especially if it's one of the women alone." While we couldn't fault their reasoning, Dewitt and I did not buy another car phone.

Neither couple is right or wrong—both viewpoints are equally valid. What is important to notice when we look at intimate relationship is the instinctual focus of attention.

Partytime for the Subtypes

Let's look at an everyday example of the subtype or instinctual behavior playing out. Various responses to the prospect of attending a party might illuminate the different habits of attention for each of the three instincts or subtypes. Notice where attention might be focused for each. Do you resonate with any of these viewpoints?

Self-preservation subtype: Focus of attention on personal survival, comfort, and safety.

I'll bring my own drink, because they might not have the one I like. I'll go early to make sure I get some of the good food. I'll park in a well-lighted place so the car is safe. I need to monitor how long I stay—want to make sure I get home in time to get enough sleep before tomorrow. I want to be sure there is at least one person I know, so I'll feel comfortable or safe.

Social subtype: Focus of attention on social interaction, one's place in the "herd."

I plan to talk to as many people as I can. I'll arrive just a little late—it looks bad to be the first one there. I hope it will be a big party—I'll enjoy seeing everybody I know and meeting some new friends. I hope we'll dance or play games. Maybe I can hook up with some people who might like to work together on a cause, event, campaign, etc.

One-to-One subtype: Focus of attention on intense interaction, one person at a time.

I hope one of my good friends is there. If not, I know I'll pick out the most interesting-looking person and strike up an intense discussion. I hate chitchat—if I can't share on a profound level, I'd rather not interact. I can always find one or two people with whom I can get deeply engrossed in conversation.

Did any of the above descriptions sound familiar? Could you begin to see yourself? Your spouse or partner? Your closest friends?

Just by this brief look at the preoccupations of the different subtypes, you can anticipate inevitable misunderstandings for couples with different approaches. Couples of the same subtype share a similar focus on the primary instinct important to them. Do I mean that couples who share the same subtype won't have conflict or misunderstanding? Certainly not! It may be just one area where they are in sync. Bringing light to bear on the subtypes and how they work is yet another way of deepening understanding and honoring one another through the Enneagram.

When Love Is Not Enough

We want to build a life together—we want to mate. But what does it mean—building a life together? For each of the subtypes, it can mean very different things.

For self-preservation subtypes, our primary relationship revolves around creating a haven, growing a secure present and future, providing for self and family. This subtype is focused on satisfactory survival.

For social subtypes, building a life together means sharing mutual interests and activities—doing things together. Social interaction and concerns, group or societal commitments are a focus for the social subtype.

For one-to-one subtypes, intimate relationship is about merging together—sharing one's deepest thoughts and exploring emotions. One-to-one subtypes prefer intimate time alone with their significant other, gazing into their eyes, attempting to get as close as they possibly can.

Subtype Collisions

You begin to see where friction might build if intimates or partners inhabit different subtypes or instincts.

Paul is a Nine who heads a center that works with children from traumatic family environments. His fiancee, Shawnee, is a Six and a child psychologist at the same center.

Working with their own types in relationship, Paul and Shawnee arranged for me to teach an Enneagram class for the staff at the center, to assist them in working with the children. It was a great success, and we went out to dinner after the workshop concluded.

Shawnee and Paul mentioned that their upcoming wedding had created a great deal of stress and for the first time in their long relationship, they were fighting on a regular basis. They put it down to nerves, but it was clearly troubling to them. We talked mainly about inconsequentials throughout the rest of dinner.

Suddenly, Paul whipped his head around to Shawnee and snapped, "Why are you staring at me like that?" Shawnee, who'd been dreamily gazing at him, widened her eyes in surprise. "I just like to look at you—I love you so much, I can never get enough of looking at you." Seeing the conflict in views, I quickly outlined the subtypes for Paul and Shawnee, an advanced part of the Enneagram they had not learned. Paul lost no time in identifying himself as social while Shawnee declared her attention to be focused primarily on one-to-one relating.

They explored their differences together and talked about ways to honor one another. Paul explained that it sometimes felt intrusive to him to be "pinned like a butterfly" with Shawnee's loving gaze. Shawnee is learning to break her gaze away at intervals to give Paul breathing space. Shawnee expressed her need for intimate connection time where they are focused completely on one another. Paul felt he could come through with "intimacy time" if he didn't feel it wasn't expected of him every moment of the day.

The common language of the Enneagram gave them a way to speak about some very sensitive issues in their relationship, without judgment or rancor. It aided them in their commitment to understanding and honoring one another.

Without the understanding of the instinctual types or subtypes of the Enneagram, we can see the first wedge being inadvertently driven between two loving committed people by their unconscious worldviews. Remember, it is ultimately the little things that make or break our relationships. Understanding of the subtle differences in our worldviews

can offer us enormous space to honor our partner and nurture our origi-
nal connection.

Mary, a one-to-one subtype Three, was dissatisfied in her
marriage to Jack, a self-preservation subtype Eight. Although
they got along very well, Mary craved more intimacy and connection in their relationship. To Mary, love meant evenings
spent looking into one another's eyes, sharing their deepest feelings and dreams, merging souls. It wasn't happening.

Jack felt their marriage was great: totally connected and
happy in the beautiful home and family they had built together.
In the evening, often Jack would cook a wonderful dinner, encouraging Mary to put up her feet and rest. Nurturing her
survival needs for rest, food, and comfort, was his way of expressing his love and intimate connection with Mary.

Feeling dissatisfied and restless, Mary went looking for the
connection she felt she needed. She found Bill, another one-
to-one subtype and a Four. Mary was convinced she'd found
the intimacy she'd craved for so long. While lost in the confusion of whether to leave her husband or stay, she came to learn
the Enneagram. "What I found was that I had confused a similar worldview with true connection . . . and drama, which I
confused with intimacy. The Enneagram gave me a way of mapping what I was seeking and doing. When I looked clearly at
myself and my husband, Jack, I realized that we really are
soulmates. I could only see that when I stepped back from the
automatic mode of the One-to-One subtype. I ended my relationship with Bill, and went back to where I really wanted to
be.

"I still need the juice of that One-to-One connection in
my life," explains Mary. "I've found it with good female friends
. . . and as Jack understands more, he tries to meet me halfway,
while I now see the deep love and caring he shows in his cooking and nurturing. I've learned to value his expression of love
more."

This divergence of the instinctual worldview nearly resulted in disaster for Mary and Jack's marriage. Having a framework or map for
looking at our instinctual habit or worldview can be invaluable in pre-

venting such a calamity. Discovering and stepping back from our sub-type bias can help us in forging stronger, more honest bonds with our loved one. Understanding our intimate's subtype bias aids us in honoring, even celebrating, his or her reality.

Honoring Another's Reality

How can we honor our spouse's or partner's subtype? In what way can I meet my intimate halfway, when his instinctual worldview is so different from my own?

Like so much of the Enneagram work, it is simple, not easy. But we can learn to shift our worldview yet again in relation to the instinctual types or subtypes. This will have the added benefit of strengthening those instincts that are less used, so we eventually have a chance to access all three equally. When attempting to shift worldviews, simply focus attention as your partner would vis-à-vis their subtype. Regardless of what issue you are contemplating or working with, start by repeating the appropriate synopsis of instinctual worldview below.

Self-Preservation: The most important thing in life is to have survival needs met. There needs to be enough rest, food, water, security. I need to feel safe and comfortable.

Social: The most important thing in life is to make a contribution, to effect social change, to be part of a larger whole, to be a part of group energy for work and pleasure, to know where you stand as a part of a group.

One-to-One: The most important thing in life is fusing with another; sharing intimate thoughts, dreams, secrets, feeling bonded with or part of another. Intense connection is lifeblood to me.

Focus your attention in your partner's automatic subtype mode. Approach the issue you are discussing or working on from that viewpoint. How does the situation appear different from this perspective? What is the best course for right action and honoring your partner? The subtype energies are basic human instincts, so it may take practice to divert your attention from your own habitual mode.

Brian, a self-preservation One, and Dana, a one-to-one Four, have been married for twenty-two years. They've built a wonderful life, creating a healing arts and retreat center together at the point they meet in their secondary subtype—social.

For Brian, most of the energy of his drive goes down the current of self-preservation, while a significant portion of what's left goes down the social current. He has a small trickle down the one-to-one relating stream. Dana diverts most of her energy down the one-to-one channel, some down social, and a trickle down self-preservation.

In their work life and commitment, they are strongly bonded in the mutual cause of providing a center for intentional living and learning. Yet the misunderstandings brought about by the collision of their primary instinctual subtypes continue to plague them.

Recently, they asked to learn about the subtypes, since their problems did not seem to be related to a One-Four clash. After self-identification of their subtypes, they wondered how they might inadvertently dishonor one another. Dana related that she often eats off Brian's breakfast plate rather than making one for herself. "That really bugs me!" burst out Brian. "But that's so intimate, sharing the same plate," Dana explained the one-to-one view. The same event was weighted strongly for both of them, trying to accommodate their automatic instinctual worldview.

In pulling back and adopting each other's worldview, Dana noticed how a self-preservation concern with whether there would be enough food for survival could be further triggered by her eating off Brian's plate. She was able to articulate that she wanted to feel connected and special to him, and he was able to find time to spend cuddling and just being with her. They feel their relationship is still a work in progress and continue to use the Enneagram in breaking their automatic habits, and learning to truly honor one another. They are taking small sacred steps.

Ellen relates a story about honoring and the Enneagram subtypes in relationship.

Ellen is a social One married to Russell, a one-to-one Eight. She sometimes finds his focus on one-to-one relating overwhelming and would sometimes prefer to enjoy the company of a group of friends. As an Enneagram teacher, she expects a lot from herself, including understanding, so she tries hard to meet her husband's need for intimate merging.

Her birthday was coming up. Russell said he'd like to do something special, to go back to the restaurant where they'd met, have the same table, etc. Ellen agreed readily and looked forward to their evening.

The night came, they dressed up and arrived at the restaurant. But when they walked in, people were sitting at their special table. Not only that, it looked like they had just gotten their appetizers, so it would be a while before they finished and left. Russell determinedly walked her past the table to a door in the far back. As she was asking what was happening, they entered a roomful of her friends. Ellen's eyes filled with tears, as she realized her one-to-one husband had orchestrated her dream birthday, honoring her more deeply than she'd ever expected.

Understanding one another in relationship requires only small shifts in perspective that allow us to see the world from our intimate's view. We can then find ways to communicate and act that honor our loved one's country and its subculture. As we become experienced travelers open to other cosmologies, we expand our own horizons by exploring the lands inhabited by those closest to us.

CHAPTER 7

The Enneagram and Family– Mothers and Daughters, Fathers and Sons

While they often look and act like their peer group and try to fit in, young people questioned one-on-one disclose a clear picture of their personality untainted by their particular peer group. We have to ask them who they are to themselves. How do they feel, act, think? What is most important to them? What do they look for in a friend? What do they fear? What do they desire? What we are really trying to ascertain is their internal worldview.

Exploding Myths About Personality and Children

When I first learned the Enneagram, the prevailing wisdom held that our personality wasn't fully in place until our early twenties. Thus, it was pointless and even damaging to attempt to "type" one's children. As a parent and Enneagram teacher, I have subsequently found this just isn't true. Children eleven years of age and older seem as quick to understand and discover their type as any adults with whom I've worked. (Many times, they are quicker to find their types—they don't seem to have hidden themselves as deeply, to fit into societal norms.)

A caution: It can be as damaging to type your kids and mold them to fit that type, as it is to mold them to fit our worldview, an unconscious practice that has been going on for millennia. In other words, don't be too quick to type your kids. Just respond to the is-ness in the moment. If your child is exhibiting Three-ishness, respond to that—make sure they know they are valuable for who they are, not just for what they do. Allow a fluid environment where your children can grow into themselves. And as they become more interested in who they are, you may share the Enneagram with them. Let them discover their own types. It will be more accurate, and it will mean more to them.

Another myth about young people came out of the prevailing Enneagram wisdom at the time I first learned it. We were told that kids couldn't type themselves because they had little or no inner observer. After fifteen years, I have found that teens and preteens often are clearer and more informed about their worldview than most adults. Almost archetypal in their presentation of type and their internal terrain, they don't seem to have grown as many obscuring layers as those of us who've worked and lived in "society." They haven't yet had to adapt themselves as much as adults.

I often use teens on my Enneagram panels, asking them to speak from their own experience of themselves. These young people tend to be honest, clear representatives of type, free from jargon or knowing too much about the Enneagram. They are more convincing to me (and my audiences) than any other exemplars that there *are* nine predominant worldviews. I am grateful to every one of them for sharing their internal landscape so openly.

Learning From Our Children

As parents, we all want the best for our kids. We want them to be successful in life and love. We want them to be happy and fulfilled. We want them to reach their full potential. And yet, all of these desires are filtered through our own perceptual bias. What "successful" means to us may be very different from our children's definition and experience of success. What is their full potential? Is it becoming like us? Something we didn't become? And what is happiness to us? To our children? The use of the Enneagram map as a way to understand our children's reality is the single most powerful daily life application I've found. And my teachers were *my children*.

Although I knew I would *use* the Enneagram with my children, I never dreamed it would become the unifying force in our family. Four members made up this tiny community at its inception: Dad, a forty-three-year-old Three; Stepmom (me), a thirty-one-year-old Seven;

Brian, a nine-year-old Nine; and Deanna, a five-year-old, Enneagram type unknown.

We never set out to teach our children the Enneagram. But since we were often engaged in "numberspeak," it came as little surprise they would ask about it. About the time they were asking, "Where do babies come from?" they were also asking, "What's a Three again?" and "Where does Dad move to when he's stressed?"

We answered the questions specific to their age group. We always started with a short response, giving more information only if they asked for it. Initially, we thought the kids would tire of the Enneagram and move on to something else. Surprisingly, they didn't. Dewitt and I shared what we noticed about ourselves as a Three and a Seven to illustrate self-observation. We still weren't sure this would be useful to our children or helpful to the family as a whole.

Then came the day eight-year-old Deanna discovered she was a One. We were painting T-shirts with the kids and their friends. Everyone was painting with great gusto except Deanna, who was frozen in front of a blank white shirt. She kept asking, "What should I paint? I don't want to paint the wrong thing."

We began working with a simple body-based practice. I had her close her eyes and paint to music, expressing with her body and paint how the music felt to her. Even her inner critic was pleased when she opened her eyes to the free-flowing designs she'd painted.

We emphasized the positives of Brian and Deanna's points early on. Of course, that's the natural bent for a Three and a Seven. But we consciously focused on the gifts because these were our children. No different from parents who aren't using the Enneagram, we wanted them to like themselves, to grow up with healthy self-esteem. After a few years, the kids began asking about the downsides of their types. Only then did we present the pitfalls, with an emphasis on just noticing and observing our habits.

Along with their improving their skills of self-observation came the more irritating ability of parent-observation. One day Deanna observed I had not only cleaned all the kitchen cupboards, but that I was lining up the sponge equidistant between the two faucets on the sink. "You look like a One today, are you stressed?" she asked. Then she went on, "Maybe I can help you, so you won't feel so stressed." That set the overall tone of our small community. We observed ourselves. We observed each other and offered gentle feedback, when we saw the habits playing themselves out. We learned together about honoring one another without trying to change each other. Each of us had to do our own work; we all practiced noticing.

The system probably wouldn't have worked so well if we hadn't continued to put in it context. We emphasized that the Enneagram was not for stereotyping or belittling, but for taking small, sacred steps to understanding, acceptance, and growth. Brian was fourteen the first time he tried "I can't help it procrastinating about schoolwork; I'm a Nine. Nines procrastinate" as a way of shirking his responsibilities. We clarified that the Enneagram was not a copout but gave him credit for creativity. Then we sent him off to do his homework.

The Enneagram gave us a common language to discuss feelings, without judgment or emotional charge. Fourteen-year-old Deanna noticed she was having trouble feeling her feelings. "I'm a One," she said. "I need to move to Four more, I think." We allowed her uninterrupted time alone in her room and encouraged her to pay attention to her inner emotional life.

Brian watched his own difficulty with feeling his anger and began to notice that it came out weeks later at an unrelated person or event. He worked on feeling anger in the moment. One day he was fighting with his dad. Suddenly, he screamed an obscenity, ran into his room, and slammed the door. When he emerged, we all sat down to work it out. The initial disagreement was easily managed. But Brian was amazed how he felt when he expressed anger in the moment and that became the focal point of our discussion.

Self-disclosure was as important to our family Enneagram dynamic as self-observation. Dewitt and I shared our inner dialogue and feelings, hoping to model both nonjudgment and open disclosure. It wasn't easy. Deanna and Brian followed suit. Sharing our best and our worst, we began to see one another as fellow beings just doing our best to observe and interrupt habits. This opened us to new levels of learning and acceptance.

I don't mean to create the impression that we were paragons of family virtue. Far from it. We had blind spots, and some of our learning was painful. But we just had to be present with all of it. As an Enneagram teacher, I felt I applied the system well to my own daily life. Yet Brian was sixteen years old when I realized I had forgotten him. I forgot the

Nine! I spent so much time making up for Deanna's being the second child and compensating her for Brian's strong connection to his dad, that I simply forgot him. While we spent family time together, I had never made an effort to spend one-on-one time with our son.

Like most Nines, Brian was all-accepting and easy to be around. He never made any demands. Now, I could have spent years of self-recrimination, but I chose to begin from where we were and take the next small sacred step. I suggested we take an aikido class together. He jumped at it so eagerly it nearly broke my heart. Now Brian and I consciously make the time to go out to breakfast, make art, or just talk. Though I missed time that I can never regain, I'm grateful that we have *now*.

Deanna noticed her father had a hard time with the low side of Four. She internalized that as "Four is a bad place" and simply denied any movement there. She proudly announced to us one day, "I never move to Four. I only go to One and Seven." Another "Oops!" We slowly began looking at the gifts of Four and encouraging her to watch for her own deep emotional connection. She eventually came home one day and told us in a wondering tone, "I'm in Four a lot! And I like it!" She had let go of the judgment against the Romantic point.

The Enneagram has been a precious gift, contributing to the psychological health—and enriching the love—of our family in many ways. We've shared a common language that helped us explore our feelings, understand our differences, and celebrate our uniqueness. A willing curiosity to explore the Enneagram map helped each of us learn from one another, while we deepened our mutual love and appreciation.

Helpful Hints for Using the Enneagram With Your Children

1. Offer the Enneagram—don't sell it.

Don't push the Enneagram on your family; that's the surest way to turn them off. Answer questions as they arise and make sure your answers are age specific. Keep answers short, expanding on information only if interest is expressed. A good way to introduce the Enneagram is in relation to daily life. If it's useful, they're more likely to be interested. Wait for a time when your child has trouble with a teacher or friend, then gently introduce the Enneagram as a way to help with understanding.

2. Teach children about their gifts first.

Kids need a basis for self-esteem and acceptance. Meet them with what psychologist Carl Rogers called "unconditional positive regard." When they feel strong enough, they will ask about their low sides. We don't need to share the downsides until then. Remember these are kids, not participants in a self-development seminar.

The Enneagram provides a great framework for honoring kids for who they are to themselves—telling a Nine how you love their capacity for just being or their acceptance of you just as you are. It reinforces their self-esteem and they feel loved for themselves. A beneficial side-effect of reflecting our gifts to one another is that it becomes a self-fulfilling prophecy. Our attention is continually drawn to the high side, and it keeps manifesting.

3. Use yourself as an example.

Self-observe and disclose your internal terrain to your family. Be sure to highlight pitfalls as well as gifts. Model noticing and nonjudgment of yourself, as well as others. This can encourage similar openness in the rest of the family.

4. Discuss pitfalls when they are not in evidence.

Pointing out to a One that they are critical and angry may not work when they are in the midst of their frustration and "nothing's wrong" mode. Discussing that Ones may look, act, and feel like this at times, can set the stage for noticing if that happens. You're really starting them on self-observing. Discuss pitfalls before they occur or at a nonemotionally charged time.

5. Provide a context.

Put the Enneagram in the context of understanding self and others. Reinforce that the system is not for pigeonholing or stereotyping. It's not a copout. It is a way of noticing and interrupting our habit.

6. Check out observations with the source.

Don't assume because you know the Enneagram well that you know what your children are thinking, feeling, etc. Ask them. Same rules go for kids as for adults. We don't know the internal terrain of that individual, even if we know or share their point. Always check it out. Most importantly, this can be the starting point for true dialogue between you.

7. *Continue your own work on self-development.*

Your kids will learn more by who you are than by anything you do or say. Live it.

But These Aren't Kids, They're Teenagers

If it seems that men are from Mars and women are from Venus, then teenagers must be from another galaxy. And in all fairness to the teens, they probably feel that way about us too. How else could they have ended up with two aliens as parents? So we're challenged to find a way to understand and communicate with one another. The Enneagram can help both teens and parents in several ways:

1. *Common language*

The Enneagram offers us a common language to talk about feelings and behavior in a nonjudgmental, impersonal fashion. This one-step-removed way of communicating helps take the sting out of sensitive communications. When behavior or reactions are something that *Ones* do unconsciously, it is much easier to explore and resolve conflicts than when it is something *you* do that bothers *me*.

2. *Ways to temporarily remove our own bias*

As we learned with self-development in Chapter 4, when we know our own perceptual bias, we can stand back and simply observe it. Understanding our default mode and habitual response, we can choose to be conscious rather than allow the automatic mode to run us. We can choose to open a space for welcoming other viewpoints and perceptions, including those of our teens.

3. *Map to understand the reality of each other*

The Enneagram map of personality types offers us a way of beginning the process of understanding the internal terrain of our parents and teens. We have a framework for inquiry; a way to question one another about our internal perceptions and worldviews. This journey of discovery also allows us to begin to see one another as individual people, not simply the roles of "parent" or "teenager."

Often a newfound respect is forged between family members as they momentarily drop the roles and habitual worldviews to encounter one another as if really seeing each other for the first time. "Who are you inside?" we want to know. And similarly, we all wish to be understood—child, teen, parent. We are united in this desire and the Enneagram helps us begin to fulfill it. Through this learning process of mutual understanding, we begin to fulfill the sacred promise of family—to nurture our growth as full and loving human beings.

Parents and the Enneagram—Real Life Stories

As parents, we want to do our best for our children. We want to teach them how to live in the world: how to function, how to share and play well with others, how to build sustaining relationships, how to dream, and how to make those dreams into reality. Unfortunately, we only know one way of accomplishing these ends—the way provided by our experience of the world. And as we have learned all too well by this point in the book, our experience is colored by the thoughts, feelings and perceptions that spring from our worldview.

We may find ourselves in real trouble when we try to push our worldview and way of dealing with life on our children. They simply may not share our worldview. Our methods and life skills may not resonate with their worldview and may not work for them at all. And though we offer (Read *push!*) all the knowledge we've gained in our many years to help them avoid the mistakes we've made, our help may not be all that helpful. Remember it is very likely that they inhabit a different country than we do. And though we lovingly offer what we've learned with the best of intentions, we all know what road is macadamed with those puppies.

Brenda, a Three, was perplexed about her teenage daughter Corrine. After learning the Enneagram, she believed Corrine was a Nine. "When I take her shopping, she can't decide on anything. I can waste a whole day and we'll come home with nothing. I keep trying to get her to make a decision." A goal-oriented Three can be completely frustrated by such a lack of productivity.

Brenda decided to keep trying but to get her own obvious bias out of the way. She took Corrine to shop for school clothes in a city some 50 miles from home. Again, Corrine was unable to decide upon anything to purchase. As they drove to yet another store, Brenda looked over at her daughter with wonder and asked, "This is really hard for you, isn't it?" Corrine's eyes filled with tears. "Yes, I really don't want to make the wrong choice. It's so far to come back to return anything." They skipped the next store, went to lunch, and ended up having one of the best talks they'd ever had. Together they discovered that Corrine was a One, not a Nine. Her indecision came from wishing to avoid mistakes. No clothes were bought that day but a deeper connection had been forged between mother and daughter. (Corrine went on to conduct her senior high school project on the Enneagram.)

It wasn't so important that Brenda be correct about Corrine's Enneagram type, but that Brenda's own understanding of her type and bias help her drop her usual way of being and approach Corrine with openness. She responded to what she noticed—indecision—but she didn't stop there. She found a way to begin honest inquiry into Corrine's inner landscape. Sensing her mother's genuine desire to know and understand her, Corrine shared her internal terrain freely.

The Enneagram gave Brenda a way to get herself out of the way, so she could really listen to Corrine without preconceptions. She knew her daughter probably was not like her, and that was the cue to step back from her own worldview, to create an open space for Corrine to communicate her worldview.

When any of us is approached with this kind of openness, we feel it. We somehow realize we can safely disclose how we experience ourselves without fear of judgment or reprisal. It's as if we know we are being asked to share ourselves in the service of understanding and building relationship, and that the questioner's own reality has been suspended for a time.

Try to approach your own child or parent in this fashion. Activate your inner observer, as we learned to do in Chapter 4. Step back from your own" reality" and create that open space for learning about your child or parent. Ask him about his inner reality, with a sense of not-knowing and in the spirit of discovery. Notice the quality of his response and the discussion that follows. Continue to keep your perceptual bias—and your belief you already know him—from blocking this exploration.

"One of the delightful and frustrating aspects of living with a Nine teenager is that in the habit of self-forgetting, very little matters. He believes things will just work out okay," relates my Three husband. "So setting consequences for unmet goals or responsibilities is next to impossible. Here's how our interactions would play out: 'If you don't do . . . , I'll take away your car.' Brian would respond, 'Okay, I'll take the bus.' 'I won't give you money for the bus.' 'I'll get a ride somehow.' 'Then we'll ground you.' 'Okay, this is a nice place.' And on and on. It simply wasn't working to approach him as I'd need to be approached."

To break the pattern of self-forgetting, they set goals together. Two mutually agreed upon responsibilities were that Brian would call if he were going to be late getting home, and he'd perform car maintenance on a predetermined schedule. If these were not met, consequences would result. The consequences were to be determined by Brian. "It was the hardest thing I ever had to do," says Brian. "I had to first figure out what I really valued or cared about. Then I had to find a way to make the consequences have real meaning . . . to me. If Dad set the consequences, all I had to do was respond to him. I didn't have to figure out what was important to me."

Brian's consequences were "no going out for a weekend if I fail to call before deadline to tell you I'll be late" and "no car for a month if I fail to perform maintenance as per the schedule." Brian had one further caveat: "Dad can't bug, remind, or nag me about either goal, as long as I'm coming through." Both honored their commitments, and no consequences were ever required.

Teens and the Enneagram—Real Life Stories

The teen years can be some of the hardest times we ever experience. There is a natural separation from parents and family as they seek their own autonomy. Communication may diminish as the teens try to work out the world for themselves. In the midst of this growing autonomy is a desire to fit in, to be part of the peer group. Confusion about identity is further complicated by hormonal surges and emotional swings. Any tools we can offer our children to cope during this time are invaluable.

Our children and their friends who learned the Enneagram found it an indispensable aid to making sense of the world. They find a framework for understanding themselves, the first glimmer of an answer to the question "Who am I?" Most importantly, they find out there's nothing wrong with them!

The majority of the normal healthy teens I've worked with have harbored some secret fear that there was something seriously wrong with them. I remember feeling that way myself in high school, afraid to take the MMPI (Minnesota Multiphasic Personality Inventory) for fear it would show I was deeply disturbed. I was so relieved when it showed I was healthy, I could have jumped for joy. I then began to believe I really might be okay. The Enneagram gives young people a map by which to measure themselves and find they really are okay just the way they are.

We were on a camping trip high in the Sierra with our kids and their friends. My daughter's thirteen-year-old friend, Morgan, asked me for an Enneagram typing interview. "I want to find out about myself," she declared. An hour and a half later, we realized together that Morgan was a Four, a Romantic. She confided, "I always thought that I was really weird, really messed up. It's so cool that it might just be that I'm a Four and that Fours all think there is something wrong with them. That it's just part of the personality." She was both thrilled and chagrined to know there were others like her, since she enjoyed being "unique." I assured her she was unique—there is no other Morgan, even if there are a great many Fours who share a general worldview.

She was very well versed in the downside of her inner Self, so we focused on learning the gifts of Four. We looked at her strengths and where the personality might also trip her up if she were unconscious of it. We reinforced—with the objective help of the Enneagram—that Morgan was okay just the way she was, and that she had a map for continuing to grow into the kind of woman she wanted to be.

The Enneagram also provides teens with a valuable map for understanding others. It provides a way of understanding adults and their peers as individual people, with gifts and failings, with separate-but-equal worldviews, just doing the best they can. It is a profound experience for young people and adults to "meet" or see one another as equals. We are all people, all trying our best with the limited information we have on hand from our worldview, and sometimes we fail. But at least with the Enneagram, there is a framework for understanding others' "failings" emanating from the default mode, and relieving us of the burden of taking it personally.

Morgan learned more about the Enneagram and discovered that her Mom was a Six. Many power struggles had taken place when her mother wouldn't allow her to do things or go places without a myriad of backup and contingency plans. "I thought my mother thought I was an idiot or even incompetent, worrying that something terrible would happen every time I set foot out the front door. She drove me nuts."

Seeing her mother as a person with her own Six worldview running her, gave Morgan the map to realize her mom couldn't help envisioning worst-case scenarios. Her mom had to plan to keep her safe, even when it seemed excessive. At no time was she assuming Morgan was not capable or careful, just that there were a lot of dangerous things in the world that could catch you unawares. In other words, it wasn't personal. "It still bugs me, but I really understand why she does what she does," says Morgan. "It makes it easier to deal with, and I try to honor what she is going through by letting her know all the contingency plans and safeguards, even if I don't think they are really necessary."

Deanna, our One child, told us a story about understanding one of her teachers. She asked her Eight teacher a question. "Oh, please!" Mrs. X blurted impatiently. "I just got through telling you that! Weren't you listening?" Then she repeated the information again. In relating this incident, our daughter chuckled gleefully, "I just love her—she is such an Eight. She has great energy! Whatever she's thinking, you know it!"

I can imagine a much different outcome for our child who has a self-critic the size of the Grand Canyon. If she had no way to account for this behavior, she might have felt "wrong," "bad," or chastised in some way. But the Enneagram map showed her "Eights just do that" and it isn't meant personally. She has a way to put behavior in context and understand where it comes from, easily and naturally.

One of the great gifts the Enneagram can offer young people is the activation of their inner observers. To start off life with a way of observing and stepping back from one's own reality will put them far ahead of the game in understanding and relating to others. I only wish I had found it before midlife!

"I am such a One!" Deanna exclaimed. "Let me tell you what happened this week—it is so amazing. I was talking to Tina and Liz, and I said something unkind without meaning to. I told Tina that she always takes center stage when we're in a crowd. She just looked at me and then the bell for class rang. For two solid days, I replayed the conversation over and over in my mind. I felt so bad for saying that to her. I kept asking myself, how could you be so stupid, so thoughtless? What was wrong with you? And on and on and on. So I finally got up the courage to talk to her about it and said that I was so sorry for what I said the other day before class, and that I really didn't mean it the way it sounded, etc. She just stared at me and said she didn't know what I was talking about. When I told her, she didn't even remember it. She didn't find it insulting at all. And I spent two days beating myself up over it. Ohmigosh, I am such a One!"

Deanna is able to observe herself and learn when the unconscious habit is running her. She is less attached to her worldview as the only reality. More importantly, she is learning compassion and understanding for herself, seeing the inner critic as a function of her personality and not necessarily the truth.

Recently, a sixteen-year-old Four, Yanna, contacted me via my Web site. She poured out her heart with all she was learning about her Fourness. During the course of our email conversation, I asked her if the Enneagram was useful to her in daily life. Here is her reply:

"Having just found my enneagram type, I think it has been helpful to me personally. It's comforting to know that I do things and react in my own way to everything and am so unique. And I'm happy I'm a Four too, although it's kind of hard to live with, because of all my intense feeling, but I think it's really worth it. The more I read on my Enneagram type, the more I like myself.

It sounds odd, but when I read something about Fours, it's like, Yeah! That's right. I always feel like that! Knowing about this stuff is just like an explanation of who you are. It has really helped me the last few months, since I've been having a really hard time 'cause I miss Italy so much, and I know now that I just must follow my heart in whatever I do. I practically have my whole life planned out already, although I hope it takes many unexpected turns. This is something I would always be willing to learn more about."

The Enneagram map gave this young woman a way to describe her inner landscape and begin her journey of understanding herself. What if all of us had begun our journey of self-knowledge and awareness so early? Who might we be today?

Working With Our Children's Worldviews— the Nine Types

We can offer another view for our children to consider in addition to their habitual worldview. Serving as another pair of eyes for them, we can illuminate the shadow they cannot see when their perceptual bias is blocking their vision. Whether or not our children know the Enneagram, we can counter some of the beliefs which spring from the personality's automatic mode and begin the questioning of those beliefs. And no matter if we correctly or incorrectly determine their type, we can simply respond to the is-ness before us. We can't go wrong in that.

Perfectionist One: Point out the perfection in imperfection, such as in nature.

Giver Two: Focus attention on the young Two's own needs and desires.

Performer Three: Praise them for who they are rather than just for what they do or produce.

Romantic Four: Focus attention on the here-and-now—the extraordinary in the ordinary.

Observer Five: Focus on wisdom of emotional centers and mapping human behavior.

Loyal Skeptic Six: Listen carefully to fears and concerns. Offer honest reality checks.

Optimist Seven: Focus interest and fascination on learning more from pain or difficulty. Let them know there is an escape route—they can always stop, so what do they have to lose?

Straight Shooter Eight: Model the invulnerability of vulnerability no one can hurt you when you've shown it already.

Mediator Nine: Focus the Nine's attention on finding and expressing their own preferences and priorities. Allow enough time, with a structured end point.

These strategies for working with our childrens' worldviews are general starting points. They may also open dialogue and questioning that will help both parent and child learn more about one another. As we grow up together, we may connect more deeply, beyond roles and beliefs, to the essential person inside each member of the family. The Enneagram can serve as a map of enrichment and compassion for both parents and children, bringing us closer together while honoring our differing gifts.

CHAPTER 8

The Enneagram and Work–Building Sustainable Working Relationships

Our "mental models" determine not only how we make sense of the world, but how we take action.

—Peter Senge

. . . organizations break down, despite individual brilliance and innovative products, because they are unable to pull their diverse functions and talents into a productive whole.

—Peter Senge

Relationships are the heart of any business or organization. Whether we are entrepreneurs dealing with clients and suppliers or we work for a multinational corporation marketing a service to a target audience, we need to create sustainable relationships in order to be successful.

Clients and consumers are not the only venue for relationship-building. Productivity depends on the quality of relationships between departments, managers, coworkers, and subordinates. Understanding how our bosses, coworkers, or employees come at the world makes it possible for us to find a common meeting ground, and get down to business.

Yet there's a more important reason to develop good working relationships than enhancing productivity or being successful. We spend a lot of our time working. Depending on our ability to get along with others, the workplace can be a joy or misery. Good relationships enhance our work environment and make it more enjoyable to go to work regardless of what we do. Bad ones can keep us from wanting to go to a job we love.

Who Are These People?

We choose our family and our friends, but with a few exceptions, we don't get to choose the people with whom we work. The most diverse group we'll probably ever encounter will be in work and business. It is essential we have a map to guide us in dealing with this personal diversity. Many businesses are educating their workers in ethnic and cultural diversity in the workplace. Still others have actually worked with systems such as the Myers-Briggs or Personal Style Inventory. These maps offer useful information in working with differing cultural and personal styles.

The Enneagram takes us even further, giving us a view from the *inside* of another individual. We discover information critical to understanding each of those with whom we work, and the internally held worldview that is the basis for truly understanding them. We find what motivates them, their strengths and weaknesses, and how they change under stress. But we discover how to build a good working relationship through honoring their personal reality.

We needn't wait for our companies or organizations to commit to personal diversity and train everyone with whom we work. Although more and more businesses are bringing the map of the Enneagram to managers and staff, it is likely that we will be using the Enneagram on our own at first. Even this seemingly one-sided approach has a good deal to offer us in building effective and satisfying working relationships.

Get Yourself Out of Their Way—and Out of Yours

If we interact with others from our own limited worldview, we will miss the synergy good relationships provide in the workplace. Most of us have learned how to deal with others whose worldview has similarities to ours. It's not surprising to find we have the most difficulty with those whose views are greatly divergent from our own.

Probably the biggest obstacle to building a relationship with someone very different from ourselves is our personality's unconscious bias or worldview. We tend to use our own personal paradigm as the gold standard for reality, rejecting those paradigms that conflict with our own. The Enneagram can best be used as with any relationship—to get ourself, our automatic worldview, out of the way. We then have an opening where we can begin to look for and accept the presence of worldviews other than our own. Already we are much less limited.

Lucinda Hayden is a Seven with a thriving hypnotherapy practice. One of her specialized programs, Simply Stop, is designed to help with smoking cessation. She couldn't understand why some clients responded with enthusiasm to her approach and others "looked at me strangely" when she excitedly proclaims, "Quitting smoking can be fun!" After learning the Enneagram, she says, "I now try to find out more about my client's worldview and honor their particular paradigm, rather than assuming that everyone is motivated by the desire to have fun. I've completely changed how I approach my clients, depending on their Enneagram type. I try to approach them with something that works for each of them rather than giving what I would respond to."

Lucinda has learned her own unconscious bias and to get it out of the way of a therapeutic working relationship with her clients. Her clients have responded by expressing how understood they feel and by returning to work on other life issues besides smoking.

Communication Styles of the Nine Types

No matter what our position or job description, we have to communicate with other people in the workplace. Even if we only interact with others by telephone, or we only speak when we have our yearly performance evaluation, it is helpful to know the communication style our personality prefers. Each Enneagram type has both specific strengths and concomitant pitfalls to their default communication or speaking style. We naturally would like to maximize our strengths and minimize the pitfalls that will cause our message to be misinterpreted or not heard at all.

It is also helpful if we can expand our communication talents to include those of the other Enneagram types. When we can avail ourselves of different ways of communicating, we have the option of matching the style to the appropriate situation. All nine styles work well in given situations. We don't want to be limited to our personality's default mode, when another style may work better. In examining the speaking styles of each of the nine Enneagram types, it is good to remember that when you get lost in your own story (personality), you lose eight-ninths of your listeners. If you speak from your strengths or gifts and allow these to serve the message, they'll hear you.

Perfectionist One

Speaking Style: Sermonizing

Strengths: Honesty, integrity, doing it well, getting it right, detail-oriented. Wants to be good.

Pitfalls: Can preach or sermonize (Because it's right!). Can get so caught up in the details they lose their listeners or don't ever do a speech because it isn't right yet. Can be inadaptable so never change their message for fear it will be wrong.

Recommendations: Be in service of the message rather than being right. Know when it is good enough. Don't preach or sermonize, there really is more than one right answer; they'll turn you off if you preach anyway.

Giver Two

Speaking Style: Warmth

Strengths: Empathy, a caring compassionate bent, orientation toward relationship and service. Ability to connect quickly.

Pitfalls: Pride in all of the above (I am giving you so much, so be grateful). Over-emoting. Get lost in the emotional stories and lose the audience. Shapeshifting to be liked—can seem wishy-washy.

Recommendations: Humility—these folks were doing okay before you got here. Give the best you have to offer without attachment. Use stories in service of the message. True empathy involves knowing when to back off. Just because you believe you know what they need doesn't mean they want it.

Performer Three

Speaking Style: Convincing

Strengths: Ability to sense what the audience wants and shift/change message so it will be heard. Can sell anything. Charming and facile. Quick. Inspirational. Usually very good on stage.

Pitfalls: May not have own message. May be strong on style and low on content or actual message. May seem too slick, too polished. Audience doesn't trust. Can cut corners and slide through. Pretend to know more than do.

Recommendations: Be clear on your message; don't cut corners but learn your topic well. Figure out where you stand so you don't lose your Self in trying to be successful at speaking. Give credit to others.

Romantic Four

Speaking Style: Lamenting

Strengths: Unique point of view, dramatic, often very skilled on platform in delivery, sensitive and creative. Emotional.

Pitfalls: Can be overly dramatic; can be so attached to uniqueness that audience doesn't relate. Can be lost in the emotion lamenting that they lose the audience, like the Two.

Recommendations: Use drama to accentuate your points; if it doesn't enhance the message, get rid of it. Ask others you trust if you've got too much drama, emotionality that do not serve the message. Be wary of separating yourself from the audience—unique, so they could never hope to be like you.

Observer Five

Speaking Style: Dissertation

Strengths: Depth of knowledge about a topic, often are the expert in what they speak on, ability to observe acutely and describe well, superb humor—often dry, well-read—will probably know what all others have said/written on the subject. Can systematize information well.

Pitfalls: Can have speaking style of dissertation. Can quote everybody and not reference self. Can seem detached or not present; may withhold information. May give too much information and wander the labyrinths of the mind.

Recommendations: Watch for quoting too many, too much (As Plato said; as Clinton once said . . .). Quote yourself. Pare down information to what really serves the message; not everyone wants to explore it to the depth that you do. Be present while speaking. Use observing and humor skills. Simplify.

Loyal Skeptic Six

Speaking Style: "Shotgun" or apologetic

Strengths: Loyalty, duty to people or a cause, especially underdogs; healthy skepticism, can sense hidden agendas, prefers group to spotlight often. Anti-authoritarian.

Pitfalls: Doubt own message, so they are unclear; push cause down others' throats. Can be overly pessimistic—doom and gloom if you don't change, senses hidden motives and danger where there are none. Can use shock techniques due to ambivalence toward authority. Talking in short shotgun blasts.

Recommendations: View yourself as in service to the underdog cause of the message. That means clearly defining what the message is. Don't try to shock or bring out listeners' true feelings. Slow down speech, learn the pause. Highlight an optimistic feature. Don't push causes— illuminate them. Trust yourself—don't apologize.

Optimist Seven

Speaking Style: Enthusiastic storyteller

Strengths: Storytelling, humor, optimism. Great reframers—of everything. Upbeat high energy people who emphasize work, etc., as fun. Can draw parallels and similarities between distinctly different things. Adventurous, enjoy life to the fullest.

Pitfalls: Can become too attached to own stories, can make a story out of a mundane trip to the post office, which may not be relevant. If you seem pollyannaish to audience, they won't trust you. Overemphasis on fun may lose audience. Can be dilettantish—know a little about everything, but not a lot about any one thing. Can use too much humor.

Recommendations: Learn the topic really well—don't get distracted by other things. Use humor and stories in service of the message. Don't reframe everything—take a beat first. Insert a little downside, then the plan to deal with it. Be sure the parallels and connections you make are relevant and helpful.

Straight Shooter Eight

Speaking Style: Commanding

Strengths: Clear, direct, straightforward. Forceful. Able to communicate message by pure determination. Honest and just. What you see is what you get. Good at direction—inspires by sheer will. Large energy and presence. Instinctual knowing—from the gut. Clarity.

Pitfalls: Too in-your-face—pushy, bull in a china shop. Too attached to "My truth is *the* Truth" and there is no room for any argument. Too little backup information. I know from my gut.

Recommendations: Filter speech through heart and mind. Consider impact of speaking, recommendations, etc. Recognize dissenting points of view—and allow them. Do homework to back up instinctual knowledge and flesh it out.

Mediator Nine

Speaking Style: Epic, conciliatory

Strengths: Able to see all points of view and hold them equally. Merges with audience energetically—we are all one. Nonthreatening, comfortable. Easygoing charm.

Pitfalls: Epic Nine way of speaking. The speech has no point, holds all points of view without a conclusion. Can have laconic way of speaking that puts people to sleep. Passive verbage may lose people ("How leadership happens to you . . . "), may not compute for the rest of us.

Recommendations: Define the point of the message and be clear about it. Be careful of the tendency toward passive verbage. Don't fall asleep onstage, don't go on automatic. Beware of epics—keep coming back to the point. We don't need the whole story.

How Do I "Type" Others I Work With?

The Enneagram gives us eight perspectives in addition to our own, and a framework for understanding why people act and react as they do. We look for clues as to the Enneagram types of the people we work with and try to respond in a way that honors what we encounter. While we may not truly know their type, it doesn't matter. We can respond to the is-ness that we observe.

If we observe One-ish energy or behavior, we can respond to that. If it doesn't work, we can go back to observing and try another viewpoint. Better yet, we can ask questions from our Enneagram map (without mentioning the Enneagram per se). How do you like to be approached? What is most important to you in a working relationship? What do you like best about work? Least? These answers may not nail down the type for us, but they are the information we are really after. We are learning a bit of the internal terrain and ways to understand and honor another individual.

An Eight, Dan is a vice president in a major financial company. He worked for a Seven for many years and they developed a strong relationship. "We were alike in a lot of ways. We both used our instincts, we made decisions quickly, and we had a lot of fun. We enjoyed our work," says Dan. Having familiarity with the Enneagram, Dan used it primarily for his own self-development and with his family.

When his Seven boss retired, he found his new boss very different: quiet, reserved, often behind closed doors. "I wasn't sure if he was a Five, but everything about him suggested that was what I was dealing with. I realized my usual shorthand method of communicating and quick decision mode might seem aggressive and poorly thought out to him. So I worked on communicating with him via email first, allowing him time to think things through before approaching him. I also tried not to fill up the space when we were face to face. It was hard for me to change modes, but worth it. I believe that I would have eventually figured out how to work and deal with him. But I also believe that the Enneagram map saved me about a year of trial and error!

Dan wasn't sure of his boss's type, but he knew enough about his Eight worldview to understand how he might be perceived by others. He was able to pull back from his own bias and consider how his new boss might like to be approached. He worked with the is-ness he observed—the Five-like behavior and energy of his boss. His acceptance and honoring of his boss's apparent personal paradigm helped him take the steps to build a good working relationship from the start.

The Real Gift—Listening With New Ears

The real gift in trying to ascertain the Enneagram type of those with whom we work is a new quality of listening. Often when engaged in conversation with another, we are already formulating our reply while the other person is still speaking. When we are listening for the cues that will illuminate their Enneagram point, we listen very intently and completely. If we *never* figured out another person's type, if all we ever got from the Enneagram was this "listening with new ears," it would be more than enough to change the quality of our relationships.

Time and again, people will respond that they've never felt so "heard" as when another is trying to ascertain their type and understand who they really are. We don't need to feel guilty for having the ulterior motive of learning someone's type. Our true intention, to understand another's reality and grow a relationship, comes through. That is what people respond to. I hear from people in every walk of life, from nonprofit organizations to financial planning corporations, that each of us just wants to be understood and appreciated for who we are. This focused listening starts us doing just that for one another.

Fear of Eights–Disdain of Sevens: Typing Versus Stereotyping

While we are on the subject of "typing," we need to take a look at stereotyping. The true focus in building relationships with others involves inquiry into another's inner landscape, rather than just finding their Enneagram type. We run the risk of falsely believing we *know* another person if we know their personality default mode.

In many businesses when I initially come in to teach the Enneagram, I find individuals are legitimately concerned about being pigeonholed. (I know one organization that had their employees wear their Myers-Briggs types on their name badges. That isn't a problem unless it stops us from going further, from continuing the exploration of understanding throughout the duration of the relationship.)

Some people tell me they have learned too many systems where they felt they were on the receiving end of stereotyping, or that they themselves learned only enough to categorize others. These systems proved to have limited usefulness to them in everyday work and working relationships.

"Women are too emotional." "Men are too aggressive." It's clear to most of us in this enlightened era that these statements are gross oversimplifications and stereotypes based on gender. Stereotyping can be done with any system or way of understanding our world. We must be alert to our inner dialogue when it lapses into generalities such as "I just don't get along with Sixes. Sevens can never commit to anything. Fours are just too dramatic. Eights are scary, confrontational people." These thoughts may crop up as we are learning the map of the Enneagram and as we are trying to make sense of the reality of others. And while it may be a natural part of the learning process to simplify as we explore others' personal paradigms, we know that is not *real* or the truth.

A woman who trained as an Enneagram teacher at the same time I did, coined a phrase to describe being on the receiving end of such stereotyping. She called it "point shame." It occurs when you meet someone who knows the Enneagram and they ask what point or type you are. Then you answer and their face drops, and they walk off muttering, "My ex was that point." She claimed that it felt like all the sins of all the people who shared your point or type were visited upon you by virtue of the worldview you held in common.

I can promise you it is not a pleasant experience. The converse of point shame is "point pride"—where we are enchanted by our personal paradigm and proudly proclaim that we wouldn't want to be any other point. We list the gifts of the point as if they are automatically shining from us with no effort or attention on our part.

It's easy to stereotype based on commonalities that we notice. We add up these commonalities to create a "mental model" for ourselves. There's nothing wrong with doing so as long as we hold these models lightly, with room for new information to enter and reconfigure them.

Mental models we might hold after learning the Enneagram and applying it for a short time are "Eights are intimidating" or "Sevens can't be counted on." Sure, I've worked with Eights who intimidated me. And I've known just as many "soft" Eights who share the view that "Only the strong survive" but enact it fairly quietly. I've known escapist Sevens I would not count on, but just as many I would trust with my life. I've known Ones who were picky and critical and others who acted as my most gifted teachers.

It is important we realize the purpose of the Enneagram is to give us a broad map of internal worldview or personal paradigm. This important map gives us a starting place to begin our exploration of another paradigm or Enneagram culture. Even our mental models are simply constructs we create to help us in understanding. We have to continue to question our models, and leave room for them to grow, so they may more closely connect us to the complexity they represent.

Synergy Through Diversity

Businesses and organizations are recognizing that the strengths of individuals working together adds up to a synergy: a whole that is greater than the sum of the parts. We can actually be more effective when we combine different gifts than when we use strong people with the same gift, since there is an inherent weakness in working with a limited number of views. Self-directed work teams work best when all viewpoints represented are honored for their contribution to the whole of the project. (Unfortunately, it can take participants of these self-directed teams a long time to get to know one another's gifts if they have no map to learn everyone's worldview.) When we individually know our gifts and weaknesses, we can link up with others who complement us.

Janice is head nurse of a busy critical care unit in a community hospital. A Nine with an Eight wing, she has little difficulty making decisions regarding policy or patient care. She is competent and clearly "in charge." The nurse educator of the critical care unit, Marion, is a Seven. She knows the Enneagram.

One day Marion observed two staff members Janice likes and respects engaged in an interpersonal conflict. Janice was becoming more and more anxious, as she could see no way to keep the peace. Both viewpoints seemed equal to the Nine.

Marion realized the Nine was extremely stressed and upset, uncertain how to resolve the conflict. And since she is on the same level on the organizational chart, Marion took Janice aside and asked if they might trade duties for the morning. Janice could go to an important meeting and Marion would deal with the interpersonal conflict.

Marion recounts, "Janice's eyes widened and she said, 'You wouldn't mind?' I told her I wouldn't mind, that it didn't bother me to deal with the nurses' personality clash. Besides, I thought they could use her views in the meeting.

"Janice was thrilled to go off to the meeting and came back later to thank me. She said 'You know, that is the hardest thing for me, to deal with personal problems between my staff when I respect them all.' I told her that we could work together on combining our strengths and doing those things we were best at. We don't all have to be good at everything."

Now there's a revolutionary thought! "We don't all have to be good at everything." Marion's understanding of Janice's strengths and weaknesses as well as her own helped them work together in a way that combined the best each had to offer. Janice didn't have to perform the one task she dreads. Both were able to enjoy their workday when personal diversity was taken into account and accommodated.

Shifting Your Own Energy

Another way the Enneagram can help us enhance our interpersonal relating has to do with matching energy. Remember our discussion regarding the different energies or force fields of each of the types back in Chapter 3? We can address energy in two ways. First, we can learn our own automatic energetic and be aware of its effect on others. Dan, our Eight with the new Five boss, was aware of his own propensity for filling up space and realized it might be overwhelming for a withdrawing Five. With practice we can choose to shift our energy appropriately. How do we do that?

Exercise: Shifting the Energetic

(You might want to close your eyes the first few times you do this exercise.) Envision your force field and its boundaries. Now imagine it is expanded to fill the room. Note how your force field feels in your imagining. Picture it contracted back deep inside or behind you. Notice if that feels different. See it diffuse and spread over a large area, with a great deal of space between the molecules. Note how that feels. Practice moving your force field.

"Where attention goes, energy flows" was the maxim we discovered in Chapter 5 on self-development. That is literally true for our force field of energy. If we imagine it is contracted, we have directed our attention in such a way that it does contract. If we imagine our energy is pulled back into ourselves, it will be. If we direct attention to our head, heart, or gut—that is where our energy flows. At first we may not feel anything (except silly), but with continued practice we'll find an interesting occurrence. We will begin to feel others' force fields more clearly. I don't know why it is easier to feel others' force fields initially than it is to feel our own, but it seems to work that way. We can then begin to trust that it is possible to shift our attention *and* our energy.

Matching Energy

As we become more sensitive to another's energetic, or force field, we can begin to match ourselves to that energy. It's a way of connecting that creates a nonverbal deep rapport. Establishing such a rapport can facilitate understanding, agreement, and even conflict resolution.

Many people in business have learned the techniques of Neuro-Linguistic Programming (NLP) where one "mirrors" the body posture, mannerisms, and even breathing patterns of another to create nonverbal rapport. It's extremely popular because it works! The individual being mirrored feels understood and accepted on some level beyond speaking. Even the person executing the mirroring is able to feel a wordless connection with the one who is mirrored. Thus a rapport can be attained without a single word being spoken.

A similar nonverbal rapport can be established by mirroring or matching the energetic of the person you are dealing with. Here's an exercise that may help you become more facile in energy matching.

Exercise: Matching Energy

Be aware of the energy you run into throughout the day. Practice matching energy to the force field or energetic you encounter with the intention of creating an invisible rapport. If energy is "bigger than life," expand your own force field to meet that energy. If energy is pulled back or withdrawn, contract your own force field to make it nonthreatening. Note how your interactions seem to you. Are they easier? Different? Do you notice a connection?

Living With the Boss

It really doesn't take a huge shift of attention or energy to honor another. We simply need to meet them halfway. Somehow people sense when someone is really attempting to match them energetically, to honor their worldview: they begin to feel understood.

Mike is a Seven with a Six wing. His larger-than-life Eight boss was constantly berating him, becoming angry and yelling at him when unavoidable delays occurred or projects didn't happen as fast as he thought they should. Mike's attempts to explain legitimate problems only served to enrage his boss further. Mike was at his wits' end. Working in a group with some role play, John, an Eight, played Mike's boss and Mike played himself in a typical interaction.

Upon confrontation, Mike began a lengthy, detailed explanation of all that had happened. When the Eight interrupted angrily, Mike shrank back—and so did his energy! John glowered and moved forward toward Mike. We then coached Mike to meet his boss's Eight energy, to expand and push out from his belly. We also asked him to honor his boss by getting straight to the point, and being clear about deadlines and expectations for his Eight boss.

Mike worked on these aspects with feedback from John and the group. When next his boss called him on the carpet, Mike matched energy, stood his ground, and simply said, "The delay is unavoidable, it'll be on your desk tomorrow by ten." His boss responded, "Fine. Get to it."

Remember, Eights want someone who'll stand up for what they believe, who won't wimp out. They want someone who'll match their energy (not escalate it, or you might end up being "eaten") and come through. Respecting action and clarity, they are impatient with lengthy discussions or explanations. Mike was initially approaching his boss, both in terms of content and energy, the way Mike himself would like to be approached. But it was not at all the way his *boss* liked to be approached, so it simply didn't work.

Motivations and Rewards

Here's where the golden rule just isn't enough. We need to go beyond "Do unto others as you would like them to do unto you" to "Do unto others the way they want to be done unto." When we only treat others as we want to be treated, it may not be what they want or respond to at all.

Jane, a Perfectionist One, was working as head nurse of two busy critical care units. Six charge nurses reported directly to her: three Ones, an Eight, a Nine, and a Two. From her One-ish Perfectionist perspective, the way to reward good performance was to give her charge nurses more responsibility and more independence in policy issues and decision making. That was how Jane liked to be rewarded.

All the charge nurses flourished under this reward system except Connie, the Two. She continually scheduled meetings with Jane to go over policies or request input on decisions that Jane felt Connie could easily handle. Even though Connie was bright and knowledgeable, Jane began to question whether she was competent to handle the charge nurse job. Physicians, patients, and subordinates all liked and respected her. Jane was in a quandary: Should she demote Connie, retrain her, or just hope things improved on their own?

Then Jane learned the Enneagram and found that Twos like a personal connection and relationship with their boss. The description of Twos matched Connie. Suddenly, it was clearer to Jane. The meetings and extra time she had to spend with Connie were ways Connie was trying to establish a relationship with her. When she realized that, she asked Connie to go to lunch with her and spent time just talking about personal matters, learning more about Connie. Connie's performance skyrocketed, and Jane maintained their connection by just checking in with her periodically, making time for their relationship. These measures took far less time than when Connie was constantly trying to create a bond between them.

Giving Connie what Connie wanted, rather than what Jane would have wanted for herself, helped both of these people. Connie was able to perform well above average in her charge nurse role, and Jane didn't lose a talented staff member over a simple clash of personal paradigms.

What Motivates Each of the Types?

Often our reward systems designed to motivate others are based on that which we prefer. It can be invaluable to have a beginning understanding of what motivates each of us based on our Enneagram type.

Perfectionist One: Improvement, job well done

Giver Two: Approval in relationship

Performer Three: Approval for image or task

Romantic Four: Being special, different

Observer Five: Knowledge and understanding

Loyal Skeptic Six: Loyalty and/or security

Optimist Seven: Unlimited options and possibilities

Straight Shooter Eight: Power

Mediator Nine: Connection

Knowing what motivates each of us and those we work with can be a tremendous help in designing benefit and incentive programs. Just knowing we won't all respond to the same motivators can be a boon for managers and CEOs. Recently I was at an incentive bonus trip on a tropical isle. This trip was given as a reward to the top salespeople in the organization. One participant shared that he liked being one of the top people each year, but he was terminally bored with fancy hotels and resorts. His dream reward was to be sent to a cabin or lodge in the woods alone. He managed to make the top each year, but the incentive was actually working against him. He just did not value it. And he knew no way to safely communicate this, believing that he was the only "weird" one.

Beyond Motivation . . . to Inspiration in Each of the Types

Motivating is useful, even desirable. But most of us would like to go even further. We want to fulfill our potential, to grow as human beings, to be self-actualizing. Yearning to be inspired, we want our work to be a vocation or a calling. We want to find meaning in the large part of our life that is work. Each of the nine Enneagram types is inspired differently.

Perfectionist One: Empowerment to improve and reform

Giver Two: Making a difference to others

Performer Three: Winning—being known as the best

Romantic Four: Making a unique creative contribution

Observer Five: Quest for wisdom

Loyal Skeptic Six: Commitment to a cause or higher ideal

Optimist Seven: Visioning—work as adventure

Straight Shooter Eight: Serving through strength

Mediator Nine: Working together in harmony

Even when we know our coworkers well, even when we know what motivates or inspires them in work, we may continue to treat them as we would want to be treated. We don't lose our personal paradigm, thus we continue to filter information and observations through it. It is as if we are looking through a special pair of glasses that polarizes what we see into our own worldview, cutting out the glare from other personal paradigms or worldviews. When we haven't removed the One glasses or Two glasses, etc. from our perception, we can misinterpret what we see and hear from another. My own Seven glasses offer a case in point:

> My business partner, Nadine, is a One. When we set up Enneagram workshops, I tried to take on at least half of what this Seven considers "scut" work. Working out budgets, finances, contracts, and organizing supplies, etc., seemed like necessary evils to me. But visioning and creating the class were what interested me.
>
> Nadine told me she liked working with the details and finances. Through my too-intact Seven filter, I interpreted this as "I don't mind doing this, even though it is boring, mundane work." I continued to take on "my share," feeling virtuous that I had overridden Nadine's excessively generous nature. Finally, Nadine sat me down and said clearly, "You don't understand— I love doing this part." I had not heard her at all, preferring to believe she was really seeing the world as I did.

Assuming that others see the world as we do, and acting on that assumption can cause us to make mistakes or blunders, as I did in dealing with Nadine. Ultimately, these mistakes can be gifts to us in helping us to understand one another. Cultural faux pas give us important information as to the density and fixity of our own worldview. They help us learn yet again, that we don't all inhabit the same reality. Our assumptions serve to awaken us once again, to continue the inquiry into internal terrain, even with those we know "as well as we know ourselves."

> Nadine and I were setting up a week-long workshop in Hawaii. We had planned to explore new territory using the Enneagram as a map for transformation. By now, I knew Nadine

really did enjoy putting together the details of food, contract, etc. We worked on the flyer and publicity together. All that remained was to establish the course schedule.

We had discussed all manner of ideas over a period of months, enough to fill several courses. Finally, it was time to set the content and schedule. Even though we'd have meetings and talk and talk, somehow it didn't seem to be happening: We still had no schedule.

Suddenly in my mind's eye, I saw my One daughter Deanna in front of her white T-shirt, uncertain where to begin painting when confronted with a blank void. Maybe it is hard to start when nothing attracts the One attentional stance of improving or correcting. Perhaps it is difficult to practice discernment when confronted with emptiness.

With this in mind, I sketched out a sample schedule of days, exercises, and events for the entire week. Then I emailed it to Nadine, explaining that it was very loose—set in Jell-O rather than concrete. I asked her to make corrections, improvements, to change anything and everything. Within two days, Nadine had refined and honed the course content to nearly perfect.

When we discussed it later, we realized it is much easier for the One when there is something to correct or improve. Their attentional stance quickly sees what needs to be changed or made better. As a Seven, I work best with the blank page, where all possibilities still exist, all options are open. Understanding our separate gifts allows us to work to the utmost of our ability. Together we create a synergy, using the best each has to offer.

Dealing With the Nine Types of Bosses, Subordinates, Coworkers, and Suppliers

In addition to meeting and matching energy and honoring the general worldview or Enneagram type of those you work with, here are some quick hints for dealing with each of the types. Remember, you don't have to be sure of an individual's Enneagram type if you respond to the is-ness you encounter. In other words, go with your best guess. You'll be no worse off than you were before, when you had no map at all. And you'll begin to gain valuable information to help in growing your relationships.

Honoring Perfectionist Ones

- *Criticize sparingly:* Be careful with criticism. The Perfectionist's internal critic can take even light criticism and batter herself mercilessly long past the time you forgot you offered it.
- *Call attention to excellence:* Point out what they do well. A One is often so focused on the next situation or item that needs correcting, she forgets that she's done anything well.
- *Admit your mistakes:* Show your own failings. Perfectionists have a great deal of empathy when you do.
- *Ask for assistance:* Ask Ones for the best way to do things. Their attentional style just naturally focuses on the best method for any situation, and they are often willing, patient teachers.

Honoring Giver Twos

- *Offer sincere thanks:* Show your appreciation for the Giver's genuine contributions; do not take them for granted.
- *Establish a personal connection:* Link up with the Twos you encounter from the your heart center. Develop a personal bond or relationship.
- *Give without fanfare:* Receiving can be hard for Twos, since their identity is tied up in giving and helping. So give to them quietly, unobtrusively. If you get a cup of coffee for yourself, get one for the Two and just set it near them, without fanfare. They will appreciate it.

Honoring Performer Threes

- *Recognize achievements:* Give recognition for legitimate accomplishments and successes.
- *Don't get in the way of success:* Don't be an obstacle. When a Performer is fixed on a goal, they may run right over the top of you without meaning to. If you need the Three's attention, make yourself the goal by making an appointment. You'll likely then get their undivided attention.
- *Don't waste valuable time:* Multitasking Performers don't like to waste time. Get right to the point and let them get on with the work that is so important to them.

- *Keep the three honest:* Gently remind them to give credit to all who work on or contribute to a project.

Honoring Romantic Fours

- *Respect individuality:* Don't try to make a Four conform—it is very important that some leeway exist for them to express their uniqueness, even in a corporate environment. Eccentricity can yield creative endeavors and solutions.

- *Use the gift of dissatisfaction:* Not satisfied with merely an adequate solution, a Four will push for their highest ideal. Find ways to allow the Four to make special contributions and awaken the "heart" of the organization.

- *Don't help the four adapt:* Meet the Romantic's intensity without getting caught up in their drama. Don't try to "fix" or change them; rather, attempt to understand.

Honoring Observer Fives

- *Allow the five to work alone:* Give them space and privacy to work. Give an Observer a puzzle; they'll eagerly work out a solution. Alone.

- *Provide for ample preparation time:* Allow lead time for decisions. Observers like to know what to expect, so provide them with all the information possible, and let them think about the best way to proceed. Don't surprise them.

- *Don't overwhelm or exhaust them:* Avoid long meetings or discussions without a clear end point. For the more outward types (Twos, Threes, Eights), try not to overwhelm the Five with your energy.

Honoring Loyal Skeptic Sixes

- *Explore the worst case:* Always recognize and share the downsides or pitfalls when working with a Loyal Skeptic, so they know you are at least minimally trustworthy. Listen to their worst-case scenarios and ask for their analysis and plans for dealing with those potential problems.

- *Act as a reality check:* Without denigrating the Six's fears, act as a reality check regarding how likely a worst-case scenario is to develop.

- *Earn their trust:* Come through with what you promise. Don't misuse authority or leadership roles. Be consistent and treat others in an egalitarian fashion: Don't play favorites.

- *Allow for healthy skepticism:* Value the natural bent of the Six to question everything. It may illuminate potential problems and focus goals. Realize that Sixes may have to ask certain questions over and over, because of the doubting mind.

Honoring Optimist Sevens

- *Share the optimism:* Join in with Seven's excitement and enthusiasm, then help them realistically narrow their focus to achievable plans and goals.

- *Don't rain on their parade:* Don't force the darkside or pitfalls with the Optimist. Frame difficulties as best-case scenarios. Change your approach from "we have a problem" to "we could have a better future."

- *Open to unlimited potential:* Encourage exploration of options and possibilities which can translate into future visions and innovative solutions.

Honoring Straight Shooter Eights

- *Cut to the chase:* Be direct when dealing with an Eight. Give them the mission critical information: Is the job done? When will it be finished? What's the decision? Be clear and concise. Don't get emotional or lapse into long-winded explanations of the process or details of a project.

- *Stand your ground:* Eights don't care if you agree with them, but you must be prepared to state your case and stand up for your beliefs.

- *Tell the truth even if it hurts:* If a Straight Shooter is stepping on your toes or bulldozing, just tell them. They'll appreciate the truth more than any misplaced pampering of their feelings. Eights want feedback as much as any other type.

Honoring Mediator Nines

- *Provide enough time for good decisions:* Allow time for a Nine to make a decision, but it is important to have a clear timeframe. Work out a deadline together. Don't push the Mediator; he'll only become stubborn and passive-aggressive.

- *Deal openly with passive-aggressive behavior:* When a Nine is acting out anger in a passive-aggressive fashion, call them on it by stating how you feel. Don't ignore it and let the conflict go underground.

- *Don't discard their choices or ideas:* Don't usurp a Mediator's agenda or choice, if possible. The Nine will be angry since it took them so long to figure out what was important to them.
- *Make a personal connection:* A Nine enjoys connection with others and usually prefers working in a harmonious, cooperative environment.

Dealing With the Nine Types of Clients and Customers

A cornerstone of building sustainable relationships involves honoring the worldviews of your clients. Even if you don't work with clients per se, the others you interact with in the course of work are akin to your customers. Some organizations consider that different departments within the company are "customers" for each other. Interdepartmental relationships shift to a higher plane when departments are not engaged in turf battles, but instead look at each other as those whom they serve.

Honoring Perfectionist One

What the One wants from you: The Perfectionist client needs to know you are diligent and thorough in all that you do for them. Therefore, they may want all the information and full explanations for each detail. They need to know you've done your homework and will be meticulous. Since they value honesty and integrity, they want to know you also take your responsibilities seriously.

Potential reactivity: It may seem at times as if the One is interrogating you about every small detail. They can seem critical, as if they are judging you. Feeling they don't have enough information, they may procrastinate in decision making so as not to make a mistake.

Honoring Giver Two

What the Two wants from you: Twos want a connection with you; they want to feel you genuinely care about them personally. There will be little need to match the Two's energy: they'll match to you. Givers want to know you'll take care of them because they are special to you. And they like to be able to make a contribution to you as well.

Potential reactivity: Twos may not really hear details when you discuss options with pitfalls; they are much more tuned into their connection and relationship with you. If you must get some information across, you may need to intentionally mismatch to get their attention. Sometimes they get lost in high energy discussions and seem to change their minds midstream (hysteria).

Honoring Performer Three

What the Three wants from you: The Three client wants a positive go-getter who presents the image of success. They want someone who doesn't waste their time, doesn't hedge, or play fast and loose. They're alert to deceit or shapeshifting, since they are part of the Performer's own automatic mode. The Three wants to know that you have all the details under control but doesn't want dissertations on each one.

Potential reactivity: The flip side of wanting a Three-like consultant is that the Three is ever alert to signs of deception or selling because that's how they live. They know they can't always trust *themselves* to do the best job, just that it would *look* good. Mistrust rears its ugly head if the presentation is too slick or if any questions are brushed aside or glossed over. The Three will most likely just disappear and find someone else.

Honoring Romantic Four

What the Four wants from you: The Four wants to know you are authentic and care deeply about what you are doing. The Romantic wants to know you will design a unique program or consult with them as an individual. No ordinary, menu-driven solutions for them! The Four wants you to try to understand their special needs. Fours appreciate well-designed, aesthetic instructional materials.

Potential reactivity: If the Four feels you are trying to change them, to make them different rather than to offer advice and solutions, they won't work with you. They want to be understood, not fixed. Listening is key with a Four: to hear what they really want. The Four can pull you into an emotional reality or dream of theirs ("If only I could . . . "), but clarity of vision or what's actually needed may be unclear.

Honoring Observer Five

What the Five wants from you: Because Fives feel they have a limited supply of energy, long open-ended meetings are not appreciated. Fives do want to understand and appreciate being given information to reflect on and think about before decisions must be made. The more you can prepare the Five with what to expect, the happier they'll be. Like Ones, Fives often like having as much information as possible.

Potential reactivity: Fives can withhold information and slow the process. It may be hard to determine what they really want, if they're not forthcoming. Fives also may take time to make a decision or give a go-ahead while they analyze the data. Although they don't like to be overburdened with meetings, Observers greatly appreciate knowing you are thinking about them and are available, so check in by phone or email periodically. Fives can give off a feeling that they are superior to you—let it go.

Honoring Loyal Skeptic Six

What the Six wants from you: The core issue for Six is trust. A Six wants an authority whom they can trust. They want to know you look at the downsides and pitfalls of every situation and that you have a plan for bailout or disaster. The Six doesn't want a positive Pollyanna—to them that means you live in La-La Land and surely can't be trusted. They want to know you come through with what you say you will.

Potential reactivity: A Six may try to make you the authority and foist the entire responsibility for their decisions onto you. Or the Six will doubt your ability and authority and try to prove you are not what you say you are, questioning you in an attempt to debunk your information. (Most likely scenario is some combination of the above—so don't be thrown by it.) The worst time for a Loyal Skeptic is when things are going well. So if you are making them money or giving them what they want, it can be frightening for the Six—they are waiting for that other shoe to drop!

Honoring Optimist Seven

What the Seven wants from you: The Seven wants someone who sees the possibilities. They appreciate optimism and prefer you deal with the boring, difficult details. Seven wants to know that the bottom line is "There's a great day a-comin'" and that you see their visions for the future. They also like to deal with someone who's upbeat and fun.

Potential reactivity: Seven's overly optimistic view of life may need focus and clarity regarding any downsides. It may be hard for a Seven to focus on a vision of where they'd like to be—they see too many possibilities and options. With their monkey mind bouncing from idea to idea, Optimists can find it hard to talk about their goals or needs. They might want to make you into another fun pal, rather than their con- sultant or supplier.

Honoring Straight Shooter Eight

What the Eight wants from you: The Eight, like the Three, doesn't like to waste their time. A cut-to-the-chase plan of action is appreciated. Eights like to have their considerable energy met, without overintellectualizing and unimportant details. Since Eights appreciate the truth (even when its unpleasant), if you make a mistake, own up to it—then take care of it.

Potential reactivity: Excess mentation, emotionality, data just bores and frustrates the Straight Shooter. The Eight may confront, just to see how you work under fire, if you have what it takes to hold your ground. They won't want to be handled by or deal with someone who wimps out.

Honoring Mediator Nine

What the Nine wants from you: Nines appreciate some structure and boundaries within which to work and make decisions. They too need time to make decisions—to let the information settle and priorities be known. Give them time to mull over choices and a deadline by which a decision must occur. Appreciating their personal connection with you, Mediators need to socialize a bit before getting down to business.

Potential reactivity: Because it is hard for Nines to know their own pri- orities, they'll refer back to you ("What do you think I should do?"). Be careful not to take over, or later the Nine may reflect and decide that isn't what they wanted after all. Be sure to keep communication going, so they don't get stuck in Nine's passive-aggressive behavior. In keep- ing the Nine focused on what they want, you may need to intentionally mismatch as with the Two. Also, the diffuseness of Nines can cause a spaciness in you—stay grounded!

The Dynamic Enneagram in the Workplace— Movement Under Stress

The ability to predict dynamic movement on the Enneagram map, particularly under conditions of stress, can be invaluable whether you are working with clients, your boss, or your subordinates. When we move to our stress point on the Enneagram, we can suddenly seem like completely different people. Our behavior, actions, and reactions may seem incomprehensible to others around us, based on what they know of our usual way of being.

Jim, an Eight, is a Marine colonel. He has found that predicting how someone will react under the stress of battle has helped him mix up the Enneagram personalities to create more diversity in the front lines. Formerly, he put all his high performers, the Threes and Eights, in the front. He couldn't understand why these same high performers didn't necessarily come through both on maneuvers and in actual combat conditions. When the unpredictable chaos that soldiers refer to as the "fog of war" took over, some Threes moved to Nine and were unable to make decisions. Some Eights moved to Five and withdrew.

Conversely his "nervous Nellies," the Sixes, would move to Three and become literally heroic under conditions of stress. The warm Twos became aggressive, decisive Eights and stepped up as well. "I used to consider the Sixes and Twos wimps and move them to the back. Now that I see what really happens under stress, I find the key to working as a successful team is true diversity. This has been the most important information that the Enneagram has given me, as a leader." He also found a new respect for his staff and a confidence in their abilities.

Corporate Culture–Weaknesses and Strengths

American business is generally Three-ish and Eight-ish. Success and image are important, as are "vanquishing" or "destroying" one's competition. Both Threes and Eights like winning, like being the best or the strongest. So it stands to reason that most of us in the corporate "jungle" have a Three-ish/Eight-ish overlay. In fact, in many of the companies where I have consulted, people identify themselves as Threes or Eights based on reading brief descriptions of the nine types. It is only after the conclusion of the day-long introductory workshop that these would-be Threes and Eights separate out into all nine types.

We tend to take on the corporate or work "culture" in which we find ourselves. It feels safer—we blend in. Camouflaged in our work environment, we keep our internal terrain private. We even may suffer from the Three dilemma of believing we are what we appear to be, rather than going deep inside to ask "Who am I really?" We may know who we are inside, but it may not feel safe to let others know. It may not be honored nor seem in alignment with corporate identity or vision.

Cameron worked at a spa and retreat center dedicated to quality educational offerings that supported personal growth. The overall culture of the center was Nine. Harmony and acceptance radiated from the staff and shareholders. A sense of cooperation and community support nurtured feelings of peace in a beautiful natural setting. Simply being was highly valued (almost the antithesis of the "doing" Three).

Cameron succeeded in convincing others (and even himself) that he was a Romantic Four, a type who was easily honored in a personal growth setting. However, when under interview he revealed he was a Three. He was clear he was disgusted with his constant doing and producing, while others seemed content to just enjoy life as is. Yet as he began to find there were actually gifts to being a Three, he realized it had not felt safe to disclose who he was to the group he worked with.

He further found there were valuable contributions he could make to the retreat center by acknowledging and offering his own gifts. While it felt scary to disclose his true identity, Cameron let those he trusted know how he really felt inside. To his surprise, they embraced him and his gifts.

Knowing the Enneagram culture of your corporation, small company, or organization can be very helpful. It will tell you a great deal about the strengths and weaknesses of your workplace.

Southwest Airlines is a noted Seven culture, following the lead of the flamboyant CEO, Herb Kelleher. The main focus of Southwest's culture is that work should be fun, that flying should be fun. The company has been wildly successful in recruiting people—it was named the top company individuals want to work for by *Fortune* magazine in 1998. The reason: Work is fun. The bent toward fun has flight attendants singing, dressing up in costume, performing comic bits, and nearly always smiling and laughing. Most of the time, it really *is* fun to fly Southwest. What a change from dour, inattentive, cranky flight attendants all too often encountered on other airlines.

And yet, there is a downside to the corporate culture, as there is with any Enneagram type on automatic mode: Fun isn't always what we need. I *am* a Seven and I like fun as much as the next person, maybe more. I ought to truly appreciate Southwest's corporate culture. But there are times when I've been traveling for an extended period and I'm just tired. I don't want my flight attendant to be perky or try to make me laugh. I want to be left alone, to fly to my destination in relative peace and quiet. I don't want fun; I want transportation.

J. Peterman was a very Four-ish catalog company. The catalog made a unique statement with its distinctive shape and format. Elegant clothing and other specialty items were drawn instead of photographed. Item descriptions were embedded in small stories, embellished with drama and emotion. I longed to be a part of those stories; it was worth it to read the catalog even if you didn't order anything. If you did, the payoff was in quality. The downside? Sometimes, it was difficult to tell what a garment really looked like by examining a drawing. Occasionally, it would have been helpful to have a little more detail about the specs of the item and a little less story. (Note: J. Peterman went out of business in the late 1990's.)

Southwest Airlines and J. Peterman had in common a strong, well-defined corporate culture. There's nothing wrong in that. In fact, it may be desirable in terms of vision, focus, and identity. The upsides and strengths of the culture are enhanced by it. However, it is important that the downside of the culture be acknowledged, noticed, and dealt with to avoid the natural pitfalls of the corporate personality from surprising everyone.

Corporate Personality—Under Stress

Much like people, businesses and associations can move to the stress point under times of difficulty or change. The stress point can be a call to action and help the company weather change or it can show up as the low side of the stress point, causing further difficulties and hardship.

A series of financial downturns had recently plagued a previously successful health spa. Ordinarily, the culture of the center reflected the high side of Nine. Work and decisions were conducted in a spirit of cooperation and community-building. Guests were treated to an environment of nurturing connection, peace, and harmony. With the onset of anxiety and stress induced by the cash-flow difficulties, the center's culture reacted with the normal first reaction to stress—it exaggerated the Nine point and slid into some of the low side. Staff "stuck their heads in the sand," refusing to acknowledge there were real problems. Steadfastly, they continued to keep the peace. When certain cost-cutting measures were introduced, there was an increase in passive-aggressive behavior. Still, smiling sweetly, the staff dug in their heels, refusing to change.

The problems continued and as the stress built, the culture moved to the stress point of Nine—Six. The workforce broke into small, mistrustful, factions. Fear and worry pervaded the formerly peaceful community. Worst-case scenario thinking ran the gamut from "the center will close forever" to "they'll fire us and bring in all new staff." (Mercifully, this went on behind the scenes, and guests were treated to the same wonderful offerings and experiences as always.)

At this internal crisis time, many of the staff and leaders learned the Enneagram and their respective points, as well as the overall culture of the center. Mapping the movement under stress to the low side of Nine and subsequently to Six had staff asking the question, "How do we respond appropriately to this situation, rather than let the automatic modes run their course with no input from us?" Their first order of business was to bring the problems out in the open for everyone rather than ignoring or wildly speculating about the future. There were fireworks in some of the meetings, but that was felt to be preferable to an apathetic "peace at any price."

Next they asked for each department's input as to how to weather the monetary setbacks, while continuing to provide quality offerings and services to guests. The Six mode then became a call to action: A loyal commitment to the ideal helped all the staff mobilize their energy and ideas for fiscal responsibility and service. Through some innovative ideas and a few hard choices, the center not only survived the crisis, but flourished after two years. And it's likely, with the Enneagram map at their disposal, they won't be at the mercy of the automatic Nine mode again, helpless to create their own future.

The Enneagram map can be a life preserver for a company or organization capsized in the rough seas of change. It allows breathing time and space as you map where the company culture began, where it is, and where you wish it to go. Understanding the strengths and weaknesses of the main Enneagram culture of the company as well as those of the stress point can yield invaluable information as to the action and tools required for a healthy response to difficulties. Accessing the strengths provided by the culture's point and stress point can help a company right itself and stabilize as it sets a new course.

Corporate Personality—in Stability and Prosperity

A company can also use the map of the Enneagram when everything is going well. Understanding the comfort point can help in visioning where the company is going, how it will grow and work in good times. What are the strengths of the comfort point? Knowing them can help an organization find pertinent questions to ask about future direction and evolution. Growing does not necessarily mean that a company will get bigger or increase profits, although that is one definition. Growth may denote a shift in influence, a change in direction, or a refining of vision that enriches the company and all who participate in it. A company may create change from within rather than simply responding to change from external forces. In this way, the Enneagram becomes a map for development of corporate culture and vision.

New Business Dialogues is a company that matches talented speakers offering inspirational or visionary messages with companies and associations wanting such speakers for their annual meetings.

The company was growing in profits and influence. The small staff functioned well together and enjoyed their work. They committed to learning the Enneagram to better honor one another. They were also interested in determining the corporate culture and examining its strengths and weaknesses as a means of focusing their future vision and direction.

The staff consisted of a Two CEO, an Eight COO, two Ones, and a Four. All attended a day-long workshop and ascertained their Enneagram type. Staff interviews were conducted to confirm type as well as individual perceptions of corporate culture. Discovering that the organizational overlay was Two-ish was not a surprise. Together the staff examined the strengths and weaknesses of a Two-ish company. The biggest weakness was found to be hysteria—getting caught up in the emotional maelstrom and racing around frenetically while accomplishing very little. All felt it was exhausting.

A commitment was made to practice noticing and interrupting the pattern. Any staff member could call for a time-out for everyone to stop and breathe, collecting themselves. An enforced ten-minute pause could break the pattern and enhance both productivity and help everyone feel calmer. This worked intermittently but was a great boon for all in terms of noticing.

A potential problem identified was that of trying to please everyone: the speaker, the client booking the speaker, and the staff member working on booking. A Two-like feeling of wanting to be in service to all could lead to feeling drained or like a failure. Clarity was encouraged in matching clients with speakers whenever possible, without making promises that turned staff into pretzels. Appropriate boundary setting allowed staff to truly be of service without overextending themselves. These observations introduced the organization and staff to the process of noticing patterns, diminishing weaknesses, and optimizing strengths. And everyone felt more satisfied in their daily work and client relationships.

Besides assessing a company's weaknesses and strengths, the Enneagram equips each worker with a common language for addressing gifts and problems. It offers a framework for optimizing an organization's performance and relationships. If self-examination becomes an overall organizational process, conscious behavior permeates the workforce. Nothing could be stronger in promoting good working relationships. And when our relationships are good, it is a pleasure to go to work.

CHAPTER 9

The Enneagram and Higher Consciousness— Enlighten Up

If the doors of perception were cleansed, everything would be seen as it is . . . infinite.

—William Blake

Man's higher nature rests upon man's lower nature, needing it as a foundation and collapsing without this foundation.

—Abraham Maslow

Ego boundaries must be hardened before they can be softened. One must find oneself before one can lose it.

—M. Scott Peck

Your Enneagram type is who you are *not!* Or more accurately, it describes a very small part of you. You are so much more than a Seven, Four, etc. More even than the unique attributes that are yours alone. Your personality is like a pair of glasses through which you perceive life, others, even yourself. The glasses have a particular tint depending on your Enneagram type—a Seven tint, a Three tint, a Five tint, etc. Mine also contain a Lynette filter—with my unique view of the world. Your glasses have your individual filters as well. These "personality glasses" color who we think we are. But who are we really? Who was I before I formed a Self? Who were you?

The use of the Enneagram as a map for higher consciousness or spiritual growth is a natural outgrowth of the self-development work (see Chapter 5). As we begin to loosen the grip of the habitual personality and see that it is not *all* that we are, we wonder: Who am I beyond this personality? Who am I without this protective covering or these filters? We naturally want to make meaning of our existence: What is our place in the scheme of things? What is the meaning of life? How can I find union with the Divine? Whatever our religious leanings or beliefs, the Enneagram map helps us use the personality as a pathway back home to Essence, God, Goddess, Oneness, Universal Light, Atman, Nirvana, etc.

Enneagram theory espouses that we all came from Essence. In the beginning, each of us contained the potential of all nine points equally within. We were all one. Then we differentiated or had a fall from grace. (We took birth.) Thus we lost Essence and chose one of the nine ways of being in response to this loss. The drive or cardinal tendency of our type became a substitute for a lost quality of Essence. In this way, the personality contains the key to our specific dilemma—the map to our particular way home to Essence. The keys to the kingdom are within us, like our own little guidebook to heaven—right inside us.

We've all had glimpses of Essence, when personality falls away and we act or feel from a place that is more than our small self. These are often referred to as "peak experiences"—when boundaries blur and awareness expands and we know who we really are. We feel connected with everything, open and expansive. Pure peace and joy exist and we *know* without knowing how we know, that this is our true nature—our Self. This is our unchanging Essence.

Few of us live in Essence, however. In fact, most of us cannot even return there when we wish. We spend hours on the cushion meditating or alone in nature, hoping those moments or glimpses will grace us again.

These pursuits are worthwhile and increase our chances of experiencing Essence. But what is truly important is how the experiences of Essence inform our everyday lives. How do we make sense or meaning of our peak experiences? How do we integrate the large Self we encounter through moments of Essential connection with the small self that must live in the temporal world every day? How do we wear our personality lightly, so that Essence can shine through in every moment?

Step One: Remembering Essence

Our first step involves *remembering* that Essence is always there, within us. This sounds deceptively simple: to remember. Yet it requires clear intention, focused attention, and profound commitment. We continually forget our true nature, even if we have experienced it more than once. We get caught up in the hectic pace of daily life. In fact, the last thing we feel we need is yet another thing to remember! We can barely keep track of the absolutely necessary aspects of running our lives.

And yet, when we lose the memory of our Essential being, our life is less fulfilling. Something is missing. We lose touch with our deeper Self, our soul. Remembering our Essence infuses our ordinary existence with meaning and purpose. We feel our soul's connection to the Infinite.

So how can we remember Essence? It might help us think of Essence as being like the sun. The sun is always shining even though clouds may obscure its light. It is there even when we cannot see it. Even when we are engulfed in darkness on the other side of the globe. Similarly, Essence is always with us. Even when we have forgotten our true nature, even when our personality blocks it from our view, Essence continues to shine through us. We are so much more than our small self, the self defined by our personality, the "I" we think we are. Remembering takes only a moment of awareness, of being awake to our infinite, unbounded Self.

Step Two: Losing the "I" and Finding Your Self—the Nine Types

If our Enneagram point is who we are not, then how can it act as a map for rediscovering and remembering Essence? Each of us, depending on our Enneagram type, lost specific qualities or aspects of Essence. Our personality contains the clue to our search to regain these lost qualities; each Enneagram type contains a distortion of them within the personality's inherent worldview. Because we feel the loss of Essence so keenly, we cling to the *distortion* of the lost qualities strongly. We identify ourselves by these distortions of Essence within our personality. We believe we are as we describe ourselves. We must lose the "I," surrender our small identity, ego, or personality to reclaim these Essential qualities again. Each Enneagram type has a different pathway back to Essence, and it is mapped out in the personality itself.

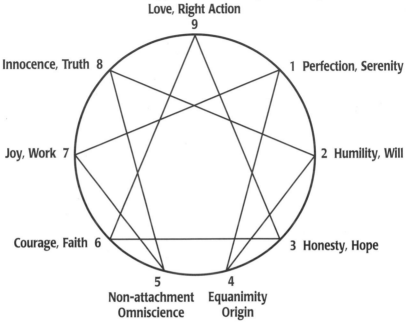

Figure 9-1 *Essence qualities—higher aspects of the Enneagram.*

Perfectionist One

Lost Qualities of Essence: Perfection, Serenity

Personality Clue: "I" am a good person.

For the One, striving to correct error, to continually improve, is a mimic of a forgotten quality of Essence: perfection. In Essential Perfection, we glimpse the inherent perfection in imperfection. Perfection simply *is*—it exists without our needing to correct or judge it. In fact, when we remember perfection, we realize that it has always been so. Imperfection was merely a construct. Our striving to correct, to reform was an echo of our true search—for the wholeness of perfection.

Many Ones tell me they experience moments of this perfection in nature. Nature is nonjudging and inherently perfect as is. It has no need to be groomed or changed. It radiates the Is-ness of Holy Perfection. This recognition finds the One experiencing Serenity, a pure nonjudging state of peace. No need to correct, improve, or reform. Perfection already exists and it has always been here. These moments of perfection and serenity are sacred openings to Essence for the One. The key to integrating this feeling is to carry the *remembrance* of this Essential Perfection into daily life, even when you are not dissolved in the Essence experience.

Giver Two
Lost Qualities of Essence: Humility, Will
Personality Clue: "I" am a loving person.

For the Two, Essence manifests through Humility as they discover it is not their personal will that brings them love when working to ensure others' dependence on them. Rather, a higher Will works through them as they serve. Twos learn to stay at home to themselves, to establish their center within themselves, rather than allowing their energy to escape through their heart center to others. Initially, this can be a terrifying experience in which keeping their attention focused on their own heart can find them with a gaping maw of emptiness. If they stay focused, however, they will find the emptiness is no longer terrifying, but spacious. Two discovers the "cave of the heart" where there is room to cradle all of humanity and more, endless potential to love and serve as a conduit for Will, acting through them.

Performer Three
Lost Qualities of Essence: Honesty, Hope
Personality Clue: "I" am a successful person.

The productive Three focuses on doing whatever it takes to ensure they are successful in others' eyes. It is very clear they have to make things happen. Often it is a failure that cannot be converted to a success that causes the Three to question both their chameleon-like deceit and their emphasis on doing and appearing successful. Doubt opens the way to true Honesty, where the Three examines their authentic desires, beliefs, and preoccupations. "What do I truly wish to do?" the Threes ask themselves, rather than "What will I be successful doing?" or "How can I spin this to make me look good?"

Often, a period of not-doing or just "being" allows the Three to realize they are intrinsically lovable and will survive without adapting or making it happen. When they realize things work whether the Three does them or not, they regain the lost Essential quality of Hope. They don't have to make everything happen, to ensure they are worthy in others' eyes! As they find Essential worth inside—supported by Hope and tempered with Honesty—they can put their talent for producing and selling in service of a chosen higher purpose or calling.

Romantic Four

Lost Qualities of Essence: Equanimity, Origin

Personality Clue: "I" am a sensitive person.

The Four feels deeply, profoundly. From the heights of ecstasy to the depths of despair, the Romantic explores the intensities of the emotional realm. Their antipathy for that which is ordinary and mundane colors their existence with flair and uniqueness, as they long for the missing element in their life. Yet they paradoxically find Essence through the cultivation of the ordinary, through the flatness of simplicity. The lost quality of Equanimity gentles and smooths out the emotional ups and downs. The Romantic discovers the extraordinary contained within the ordinary.

Cultivating the balanced energy of Equanimity leads Fours to the recovery of their Essence, where they find that the missing piece they have searched for throughout their life has always been with them. The Source or Divine Origin within them illuminates the realization that there has never been anything missing. They are—and always have been—fully complete. That which they have longed for has always been with them. Whenever they touch Essence, they remember their wholeness and completeness.

Observer Five

Lost Qualities of Essence: Nonattachment, Omniscience

Personality Clue: "I" am a wise person.

The Fives' thirst for knowledge drives them. Avarice for knowing compels the Observer to grasp for information as for a life preserver, to protect them from the reckless seas of human emotion and desire. The Five practices detachment as a protective defense, to shield them from others' demands or overwhelming stimuli. This detachment is a mimic for the lost Essential quality of Nonattachment, where being connected or disconnected are equal. Detached Fives are very attached to privacy, minimization of needs, personal space, conservation of time and energy.

Reconnecting with Essence, the Observer finds unlimited energy and potential. Through this Essential experience the Fives awaken to Omniscience, where they realize they have always known all that there is to know. Divine Omniscience fills them with pure safety and peace, with no need to learn or grasp. Their quest for knowledge ends when they discover that the wisdom they seek has always been an essential part of them.

Loyal Skeptic Six

Lost Qualities of Essence: Courage, Faith

Personality Clue: "I" am a loyal person.

Fear and doubt drive the Sixes to search for a person or cause in which they can place their trust. When the Six envisions the worst case (abandonment, death, etc.) and decides it is worth risking, they will commit with a fierce, incontestable loyalty. Though doubt and fear still exist, the Six is able to mobilize herself through certainty and bravado. Yet certainty and bravado are distortions of the Loyal Skeptic's lost Essential qualities of Faith and Courage. Certainty masks doubt and bravado is a mustering-up to overcome fear.

However, when the Six accesses true Faith, there is an innate ability to live comfortably with uncertainty, knowing deeply that everything turns out for the best. Everything will be all right, no matter what the outcome! Certainty is rigid and brittle, while Faith is open and peaceful. In Faith, the Six is comfortable with not-knowing. Loyal Skeptics can use bravado as a way to jump into danger with both feet, to put everything on the line. When engaged in action, fear falls away. Yet bravado can put the Six in real danger or foolhardy situations.

Real Courage comes into play when the action simply *must* be engaged in. Fear may still exist, yet "right action" calls for courageous measures—where clear understanding of risks exists, and action is still appropriate. Risks and fear are simply part of the equation and, unlike bravado, Courage is quiet and purposeful. Bravado is exhilarating and exciting: placing it all on the line, letting action overwhelm fear, proving yourself bigger than the fear. When informed by Faith and Essential Courage, you know you *are not* fear, and have nothing to prove to yourself or anyone else. You are simply acting as you must.

Optimist Seven

Lost Qualities of Essence: Joy, Work

Personality Clue: "I" am a happy person.

The Seven's giddy exuberance and happiness serve as a mimic for the lost Essential quality of Joy. Real Joy is a calm, quiet experience, a fullness and gratitude for whatever life offers. The Seven senses that Joy was lost and frantically works to recapture it through sampling all life has to offer, while avoiding what feels like joy's polar opposite—pain. Sadness and difficulty are circumvented whenever possible, and reframed into positives when they cannot be sidestepped.

If Sevens are lucky, they will eventually confront the darker side of life. They may come up against a pain too immense to reframe or avoid, or find ennui in chasing yet another rainbow of sensation, asking themselves "Is this all there is?" Then the whole of life can begin to be accepted, and true Joy can be seen as a combination of the dark and the light of human experience. An acceptance of "what is" can allow the Optimist to float in the peacefulness and completeness of Essential Joy. No longer needing multiple options or escape routes, the Sevens find themselves able to focus singlepointedly on work, on dedication to completion as well as process. In this, they may find themselves committing to Work that is a vocation or calling, infused with Essential Joy.

Straight Shooter Eight

Lost Qualities of Essence: Innocence, Truth

Personality Clue: "I" am a strong person.

To strong, decisive, full-steam-ahead Eights, it seems they know the truth. "Truth is important, and it will come out in a fight or confrontation. Then you'll find out what people are really made of." The difficulty is that the black-and-white-thinking Straight Shooter believes their truth is everyone's truth and everyone should see it their way. This absolute belief that they know the truth of matters dissolves when they find Essential Truth. Essential Truth is expansive and has room for holding all truths, including paradox. Eights discover they don't have the only truth, the "real" truth. In fact, their truth is only part of the larger Truth that holds all individual versions of truth. Awed by a vast and Essential Truth that contains and transcends all the small truths we hold so dear, the Eight feels a direct connection to Truth and it becomes a pathway to Essence.

Eight's insistence on having his way is a mimic of another lost quality of Essence—that of Innocence. An innocent child does not impose his or her way on others, yet is pure and clear in their desires. When a child pursues wants and needs, there is no thought of win or lose. They know what they want and move toward it with clarity, curiosity, and wonder. Getting what they desire does not mean someone else loses or that they must control the situation. When in touch with Essence, the Straight Shooter can regain this lost Innocence. Rather than controlling or needing to push their agenda, they encounter the world with the appealing freshness and innocence of a youngster.

Mediator Nine

Lost Qualities of Essence: Love, Right Action

Personality Clue: "I" am a peaceful person.

The Nine's boundariless nature leads to indiscriminate merging—a type of unenlightened "oneness" with everything. As the Nine evolves and develops a boundaried, separate self, they find they may choose when (and when not to) merge. As they connect with their individual Essence, they regain the lost quality of Essence: Love.

As the Nine regains a boundaried love, they learn to listen to their own heart's priorities as well as those of others. When Love includes the Mediator in it's embrace, they are able to act on their own behalf as easily as for others. They can differentiate and perform "Right Action," rather than drown their own priorities to keep peace at any cost. Even conflict may be appropriate and lead to Right Action. True peace is found through reclaiming and remembering these qualities of Essence.

As you can see, our personality gives us a vital clue to finding our way along the path back to an individual experience of Essence. Remembering is the key, our Enneagram type is our guide.

Surrendering Our Identity

Most often, we lose the "I" when we undergo a peak or mystical experience. One moment we are in our small self and we believe we know who we are. Suddenly, our awareness expands and our identity drops away. Time stands still and we are lost in an activity or moment.

Boundaries blur and we dissolve temporarily into the Self. We experience a merging or oneness with everything. We feel limitless peace, joy, and love. Then all too quickly, we lose the experience and are back in our small self once again. But we are forever changed by this remembering of Essence. Somehow, we know this experience is *true*.

It is also possible to inadvertently lose the small self in a life crisis or the shock of a major change. Divorce, loss, illness, or some other cataclysm may plunge us into our own "dark night of the soul." Within this shadowy period, we question who we are, where we are going, how we will go on. Ultimately, we may find we do not know the answers to any of these questions. In surrendering to not knowing, we find an opening to the boundless Self. In losing our self, we reclaim who we are in Essence.

Step Three: Cultivating Essence

"Openings" and experiences to the Self are treasured gifts that illuminate Essence within us—though all too briefly. While we don't wish to lose this communion with the infinite, simply waiting for the next peak experience seems inadequate. Can we then somehow cultivate the remembering of Essence? Fortunately, we can make a space for these openings to occur—through play, nature, and meditation.

Delight in Play

Making time and space for pure, openhearted play can be a starting point for cultivating the Essence experience. By play, I do not mean the rigorous pursuit of recreation that most of us engage in day to day. Often our play is as driven, scheduled, goal-oriented as work. Play that makes space for Essence is simply the open delight of being like a child. Watch young children for clues to losing your identity. Youngsters are often connected to Essence—fully immersed in the moment, unaware of time or boundaries, lost in wonder. Blow bubbles, dance, dig in the sand, fling yourself into water, and splash. Lose yourself in delight, as a child does. This is one of the simplest ways to open yourself to the Essence experience.

Merge With Nature

Nature is a place to nurture our soul's growth. Spending time among the trees, flowers, birds, and animals is a natural opening to Essence. We find echoes of our connection to all living and inanimate things in nature and literally feel that we are so much more than our small, tightly bounded self. Unstructured time in the natural world allows us the mystical experiences that convince us of our Essential being. We simply *know* that we are part of oneness. This nurtures our remembering in a visceral, grounded way. Even if we do not encounter the boundless, timeless state, we can sense the possibility of merging into Essence. We find our wholeness in nature.

Nature doesn't have to be a wilderness or a specific destination. Awareness can be cultivated in your backyard, the local park, or even noticing the blackbirds in the Costco parking lot. Because we know that Essence is always here, always shining, it takes very little to remember it. And the more we practice noticing, the easier it becomes.

Open to Meditation

In order for us to experience Essence other than as a happy accident, we must make a space to feel it. For that reason, meditation is an excellent vehicle for quieting the mind, heart, and body to open a space for other awarenesses to enter. If we stay inside all day working with the curtains drawn, oblivious to the weather outside, engaged in what is just in front of us, there is no room to cultivate other modes of awareness.

Therefore, we need to make time and space for allowing awareness of Essence to enter. We must pull back the curtains and open ourselves so Essence can enter our consciousness. Meditating is simply quieting the self, and creating that open space. There are as many ways to meditate or "quiet" as there are people. Some are successful sitting on a cushion and following the rhythm of their breath. Housework approached as a mindful meditative practice can be equally effective in quieting the mind, heart, and body. Gardening, cooking, making art, dancing, walking, or exercising are all excellent meditation practices when approached with specific intention and attention. When we quiet our small self, we leave the space open for Essence, our Self to make its presence known.

Step Four: Integration—Live "As If"

Throughout this chapter, we've been discussing the small personal self and the Essential Self as if they were separate entities. For purposes of understanding, we have created a model where they are "split." Yet in fact, we are both the small and large Self all the time. Essence is us even when we are not aware of its existence, just as our personality is only a small part of us even when we believe it to be all that we are. We are not just human beings, at the mercy of our personality and our environment. We are also spiritual beings, connected to all beings, our environment, and a greater whole: Essence.

So how do we bring our experiences of Essence into our everyday life? How do we integrate the small self with the greater Self? If we turn our back on our Essence experiences to engage in "real" life, our soul thirsts for remembering. We feel emptiness and loss—what is it all for? If we spend all of our time cultivating peak or mystical experiences, our temporal lives will fall apart. Bills won't get paid, work won't get done, pets won't get fed, etc. We can't live in boundless, timeless space all the time, nor can we remain stuck in the minutiae of life without meaning. How do we find a wholeness comprised of our Essence and our personality day to day?

Again, integration is simply (not easily) a process of remembering. Remembering that we are Essence can inform every act that we perform with our ego, our personality. When we know that we are so much more than our small self, it makes each small, mundane act a sacred one. We simply act "as if" Essence were shining through us. As indeed it is. It is as if unclothed, we are Essence, and the personality is clothing gently draped over us. If we wear this clothing lightly, allow it to become transparent, then Essence can shine through easily all the time.

To act "as if" may feel stilted and inauthentic. Yet that is just the personality obscuring the truth of Essence. We are not acting falsely, nor are we pretending. Although the personality, the habitual mode of our Enneagram type, is afraid to believe we are really perfect or innocent or joyful, these Essential qualities infuse our true Essential Self.

How can we act "as if" when we don't really believe we are Essence in the moment? A good friend of mine, another Enneagram teacher, explains that when she wants to open herself to Essence, she thinks "happy thoughts." In the movie *Hook*, when Tinker Bell must re-teach an adult Peter Pan to fly, she tells him to think "happy thoughts" and up he goes.

What if *our* "happy thoughts" could become reality for a short time? How would we act, think, and feel differently? How would we interact with others and our world? What would our priorities be? Try on the following happy thoughts as a pathway to allowing Essence to shine and notice how you answer the above questions.

"Happy Thoughts" for the Nine Types

Try these "happy thoughts" on for size. Act on them as best you can, whether it is for five minutes or five hours. Notice your thoughts, feelings, actions, and interactions. Was anything different than usual? What did you learn about yourself? Others? Essence?

You may want to keep track of these Essence exercises in a journal. Continue the exploration and discover how it feels to read about your experiences later. All we are doing is continuing to open ourselves to the experience of who we already are. We are noticing Essence as our deeper Self, and we are cultivating its integration into our personal self.

Perfectionist One: Everything is already perfect, including me.

Giver Two: I'm lovable and valuable without giving to anyone.

Performer Three: I'm loved for my being—it doesn't matter what or if I do.

Romantic Four: Nothing is missing—everything I've ever wanted or needed is here.

Observer Five: I already know everything—and always have. I have enough.

Loyal Skeptic Six: I've always been safe—things always work out for the best.

Optimist Seven: Joy is in the present moment—I find it in the dark and the light.

Straight Shooter Eight: I am strong enough to be vulnerable and free as a small child—I am not in control.

Mediator Nine: I am important—I am awake to myself.

When we believe Essence informs every moment, we'll see the light shining in ourselves. And we'll begin to see it in others as well. Even when they are unable to see for themselves that Essence is their nature, we will notice it. We begin to see beyond the personality, beneath it to the sweet, fragile beings we all are. Our defenses are merely that, defenses and coping strategies, and when we see through them, we feel a genuine affection for our fellow human beings. We see who we really are—Essence unbounded. We find our connection with one another and with the Divine.

Oh sure, we'll forget we are Essence for blocks of time. And then we will stop and remember. It is a process, not a goal or destination. We will remember and forget, remember and forget, ad infinitum. But with practice and cultivation of awareness, our memory will improve. Then we will find life is richer and fuller, when we infuse all we are and do with our Essential Self.

Essential Stories

Stories of Essence abound when people are asked if they've ever experienced a peak or mystical moment. Most begin by saying "I've never told anyone this before, but . . . ." We need to tell one another our stories. By exploring our experiences and their respective meanings and creating a common language for the indescribable—the mystical, the Essential experience—we can help one another remember who we truly are, individually and collectively.

Vicki, a Seven, was traveling down the Colorado River through the Grand Canyon on a commercial dory trip. "We were going through our last rapid of the day, when our boat flipped over and all went dark. At first I felt panicked and struggled for the surface. I was being circulated around like in a washing machine and couldn't get up to get a breath. After what seemed like hours, probably seconds, I looked up and saw light through the water. I was overcome by an overwhelming sense of peace and the purest, all-encompassing feeling of love. It was beautiful and transcendent. I remember thinking, 'Oh, this must be what it's like to die. It's unspeakably glorious!'

"I don't know how long this lasted—I just knew that all was love and that I was part of it too. I've never felt so perfectly at peace in all my life. And suddenly, it was over. I'd washed out of the hole and was gasping for breath. Someone pulled me into the rescue boat. My nose was broken, and I was bruised and crying. I never told anyone that I was crying because I had to leave that glorious feeling—being dissolved in love. But I haven't lost it. All I have to do is think back for a moment and I remember it so clearly. I know it was the most real thing I've ever experienced. I can always bring it back to me in the moment and feel a hint of that perfect connection."

Helen, a Five, recalls a time when she was gardening. "I was working in a bed, weeding and planting, when I lost all track of time. All I remember is the awareness of being one with everything—the soil, the warm rocks, the green shoots of plant and weed alike. The sun, the smells, me, everything was one—blurred together, indistinct. It felt like the most spacious peace. It went on forever. I was unaware of a separate me or separate anything. I think this lasted about three hours, though I'm not exactly sure. But I can feel that same peace, just by thinking back to that day. I'll never forget it."

Dara, an Eight, recalls being alone on a Northwest coast beach. "The waves were crashing and spraying, the gulls were screaming, and I was enjoying the show. Suddenly, I found myself just ecstatically romping in the surf, screaming nonsense sounds, and lost in everything. I felt childlike, yet not aware of me—just immersed. It felt like I was part of the spray and the day and everything. And there was so much life, so much joy. It felt like it went on forever—there was so much space. When I came back to myself, I felt like I'd been through a holy experience. That this was God—everything all together, all the energy fused like one."

These experiences are not unusual. They can creep up on us in the most ordinary of situations. The common elements of timelessness, vast spaciousness, and dissolution of the personal self into the boundless oneness mark these as Essential experiences. Love, peace, joy are qualities of Essence that infuse these moments and teach us what is possible when we lose the "I."

Exercise: Courting Essential Experience

Part I: Think back to a peak or mystical experience that you encountered, when you felt that the personality or small self dropped away, even if only for a moment. Write down all that you can remember about it.

Part II: Share your experience with a friend or loved one.

Essence operates from abundance, while the personality often operates from scarcity. When we wear our personality lightly, allowing Essence to permeate each moment, we are in touch with abundance as well. Coming from our fullness rather than our grasping, we have enough, we are enough. All we can do is remember, and cultivate the aspects of Essence.

We live "as if"—as if we were in touch with Essence. Then we find we really are living with Essence all the time. When Fours act with equanimity, they find divine origin or Source. When Threes act with veracity, they find hope. When Sevens cultivate holy work, they find true joy. When Sixes embrace faith, they can act with courage. When Nines act from right action, they find real love. When Ones cultivate serenity, perfection is found. When Twos embrace their humility, they surrender to will. All of these are a surrender. When Fives practice nonattachment, omniscience is revealed. When Eights lose the personal truth for a greater truth, innocence can emerge.

Exercise: Remembering Essence

To help you illuminate Essence in your life, breathe in Essence—breathe out Essence. Continue for several breaths—remembering. Notice the quality of the tasks or moments that follow.

The Enneagram is not a religion. Rather, it is a guide to higher consciousness using the clues in our personality as starting points on the journey. As such, it can be a useful adjunct to any spiritual practice. Each spiritual journey is ultimately taken alone and you will be making your own notations on the map as you go. However, if you remember you are Essence, you are a spiritual being in human form, then your path will become clearer. Godspeed.

The Enneagram and Daily Life—Making the Map Your Own

A system is only alive as long as it can give birth to itself.

—Meg Wheatley

Equipped with the many maps of the Enneagram, it is time to apply them to your own life's journey. It is important to note once again, that a map should never be confused with the territory it attempts to describe. It is a guide, nothing more. You will find your own ways of using it as you become more comfortable with its advice and its limitations.

You must make the map your own, bring it to life. The Enneagram is changing and growing still—as we learn more about ourselves and others. This keeps it alive and useful to us. But don't take my word for it, or that of *any* teacher or expert. Internalize it. Find out what works for you and what doesn't. Share what you learn, self-disclose, and ask questions of those who inhabit the nine Enneagram points at the Gathering Place Bulletin Board on my Web site at www.9points.com. Drop me a note there—I'd love to hear from you. Let me know how the map(s) have been useful to you—and how they have failed. Let's keep the knowledge alive and dynamic by sharing our stories.

The Enneagram is an experiential map. Live it! And when it has outlived its usefulness, discard it. One day, perhaps, we'll no longer need such maps. One day we may be so familiar with the territory that we may meet and know one another without needing a guide to help us forge relationships. I hope I'm around then. But until then, the Enneagram will help me map my way. I trust it will enhance your journey too.

APPENDIX I: **GLOSSARY OF TERMS**

Attentional Stance: Refers to the habitual or unconscious place that attention is normally directed for each Enneagram type. For example, the attentional stance for One is "What is right or wrong? What needs correcting?" in the environment, in relationship, in oneself, etc.

Center: (see Energy Center, Intelligence Center)

Default: (see Mode, Automatic, Default or Unconscious)

Diagram or **Enneagram Diagram:** A series of interconnecting lines within a circle that map the movement of each type under stress and in times of security. The circle, a symbol of wholeness, contains all of the nine Enneagram points.

Energy Center: Organ of perception and intelligence in addition to our accepted five senses through which we take in information and react to our environment and the people in it. We take in vital information through three additional "senses" or *centers of intelligence*. These centers are indispensable to understanding how we develop a worldview. The three centers are the head or visionary center, the heart or emotional center, and the gut or instinctual center. All humans have all three centers of intelligence, although we may not access each of them equally. Enneagram types Five, Six, and Seven use primarily the head center. Two, Three and Four share the heart as the primary center or *organ of perception*. The gut is the primary center for types Eight, Nine and One.

Energy, Matching: We can begin to sense the energy or "force field" that surrounds each person we encounter. As we become aware whether

215

someone's energy is "larger than life" or "nearly invisible" or "jabbing and retreating," etc., we can begin modify our own force field to "match" another individual's field. This creates a nonverbal connection and rapport, and can serve as a beginning to understanding.

Energy, Shifting: As we become aware of the energy of each of the energy centers or centers of intelligence, we can begin to shift our attention and hence our energy to the appropriate center for a given situation. For example, if threatened, we may wish to shift to our gut where we can sense danger, and react appropriately. If we are visioning a new company, we may wish to shift our attention and energy to the head center to create a dream, and prepare for potential problems. If we are having a sensitive discussion with a friend or loved one, we most likely will want to shift our attention and energy to our heart, to connect and empathize.

Essence: The Divine in each of us, the Essential part of us that is the same as everyone of us. This part is unchanged and unchanging. It is who we are when we strip away the personality and all that we identify as who we are separate from others. Also can be called Atman, God, Consciousness.

Habitual: Thoughts, reactions, feelings, and patterns that occur without our conscious awareness. We seem to have no choice in the matter—they just happen. Each Enneagram type has a set of identifiable patterns that play out until we become conscious of them and can choose whether or not to react in the"same old way." For example, the Seven has a "habitual" mode of focusing on the silver lining in every dark cloud, often missing the fact that there is a cloud.

Higher Consciousness: An expanded awareness where we realize we are much more than our small separate self, where we connect to the boundless experience of essence.

Inner Observer: The nonjudgmental "watcher" inside each one of us who notices our actions, thoughts and feelings. The inner observer can be exercised and strengthened to help us notice when we are being "run" by our personality, so that we may have the choice whether to continue old patterns or institute new ways of thinking, feeling, and acting.

Intelligence Center: (see Energy Center)

Internal Terrain: Our inner landscape or reality—how it feels to you to be you, how it feels to me to be me. Each of the nine Enneagram types has a mappable internal terrain related to his or her type. Beyond type is the unique internal terrain of each individual.

Matching Energy: (see Energy, Matching)

Mirroring: A term from Neuro-Linguistic Programming (NLP) that refers to the subtle mimicking or "mirroring" of body posture, gestures, breathing rate, and rhythm of another person to set up a nonverbal rapport or connection.

Mode, Automatic, Default, or Unconscious: Our habitual pattern or mechanism of being. Our default mode is the built-in mode of the personality. It takes over automatically when we are not conscious of our internal terrain or worldview, or when we are not aware of what drives us.

Oral Tradition™: Founded by Helen Palmer, the Oral Tradition™ Enneagram relies on the presentation of type by panels of exemplars drawn from each of the nine Enneagram points. Careful questioning of the exemplars reveals the basic attentional stance and the chief preoccupations of the "habit" of the type. Also revealed are ways of growing beyond type—breaking the habit. The Oral Tradition™ ensures the accuracy and validity of the stories about type by exploring type with those who inhabit the nine different worldviews of the Enneagram. Helen Palmer and David Daniels, M.D., hold professional training classes for certification in the Enneagram in the Oral Tradition™. There are more than a hundred certified teachers in the Oral Tradition™ in the U.S. and across the world. For more information, email me at lynette@everydayenneagram.com.

Personality: A collection of traits, characteristics, beliefs, and ways of perceiving, acting, and being that make up who we believe we are as individuals.

Point, Enneagram: Synonymous with Enneagram type. Also refers to position of type or point on the Enneagram diagram.

Reality: Events, circumstances, environment, and the perception of same as seen through the filters of our Enneagram type or personality.

The ultimate oxymoron may be "objective reality," since we all seem to see such different versions.

Stress Point: The Enneagram point we access that influences us in addition to our home point under conditions of stress.

Security Point: The Enneagram point we access that influences us in addition to our home point under conditions of stress.

Shifting Energy: (see Energy, Shifting)

Subtype: Related to the dominant instinct or instincts that drive us in addition to our Enneagram point. The instincts are the instinct for Self Preservation, the Social instinct, and the instinct for One-to-One Relationships. Subtype differences can have a profound effect in intimate relationships.

Type: Our Enneagram type is our personality, one of the nine described in this book. Also called Enneagram point.

Wing: The Enneagram type or point on either side of our home point on the Enneagram diagram flavors our personality. We "add" a bit of the traits, worldview, and energy of our wing point(s) to our Enneagram type.

Worldview: Just as it sounds—the view of the world that we have. Each of the nine Enneagram types has a very different "worldview." All are correct, but all are limited and illuminate only a small piece (one-ninth) of the world.

APPENDIX II:
ENNEAGRAM TYPE DESCRIPTIVE NAMES

(Author credit in parentheses)

Type One: the Perfectionist (Helen Palmer), the Reformer (Don Riso and Russ Hudson), the Idealist (Lynette Sheppard), the Achiever (Kathleen Hurley and Theodorre Donson)

Type Two: the Giver (Helen Palmer), the Helper (Don Riso), the Empath (Lynette Sheppard)

Type Three: the Performer (Helen Palmer), the Motivator (Don Riso and Russ Hudson), the Achiever (Renee Baron and Elizabeth Wagele), the Star (Lynette Sheppard), the Succeeder (Kathleen Hurley and Theodorre Donson), the Producer (Michael Goldberg)

Type Four: the Romantic (Helen Palmer), the Individualist (Kathleen Hurley and Theodorre Donson), the Artist—later changed to the Individualist (Don Riso and Russ Hudson), the Iconoclast (Lynette Sheppard), the Connoisseur (Michael Goldberg)

Type Five: the Observer (Helen Palmer), the Investigator (Don Riso and Russ Hudson), the Philosopher (Lynette Sheppard), the Sage (Michael Goldberg)

Type Six: the Loyal Skeptic (Helen Palmer), the Loyalist (Don Riso and Russ Hudson), the Questioner (Renee Baron and Elizabeth Wagele), the Skeptical Analyst (Lynette Sheppard), the Guardian (Kathleen Hurley and Theodorre Donson), the Troubleshooter (Michael Goldberg)

Type Seven: the Optimist (Lynette Sheppard), the Epicure (Helen Palmer), the Adventurer (Renee Baron and Elizabeth Wagele), the

Dreamer (Kathleen Hurley and Theodorre Donson), the Enthusiast (Don Riso and Russ Hudson), the Visionary (Michael Goldberg)

Type Eight: the Straight Shooter (Lynette Sheppard), the Boss (Helen Palmer), the Leader (Don Riso and Russ Hudson), the Asserter (Renee Baron and Elizabeth Wagele), the Confronter (Kathleen Hurley and Theodorre Donson), the Top Dog (Michael Goldberg)

Type Nine: the Peacemaker (Don Riso and Russ Hudson), the Mediator (Helen Palmer), the Preservationist (Kathleen Hurley and Theodorre Donson), the Acceptor (Lynette Sheppard)

APPENDIX III: **BIBLIOGRAPHY**

Baron, Renee and Elizabeth Wagele. *Are You My Type, Am I Yours?: Relationships Made Easy Through the Enneagram.* New York: HarperCollins, 1995.

*_____. *The Enneagram Made Easy: Discover the 9 Types of People.* New York: HarperCollins, 1994.

**Goldberg, Michael. *Getting Your Boss's Number: How to Deal with the 9 Types of People.* New York: HarperCollins, 1997.

Keyes, Margaret Frings. *Emotions and the Enneagram: Working Through Your Shadow Life Script.* Muir Beach: Molysdatur Publications, 1992.

Naranjo, Claudio, M.D. *Character and Neurosis: An Integrative View.* Nevada City: Gateways/IDHHB Inc., 1994.

_____. *Enneatype Structures: Self Analysis for the Seeker.* Nevada City: Gateways/IDHHB Inc., 1990.

*Palmer, Helen. *The Enneagram: Understanding Yourself and the Others in Your Life.* San Francisco: Harper San Francisco, 1991.

_____. *The Pocket Enneagram: Understanding the 9 Types of People.* San Francisco: Harper San Francisco, 1995.

_____ with Paul B. Brown. *The Enneagram Advantage: Using the 9 Personality Types at Work.* New York: Random House, 1998.

_____ and David N. Daniels. *The Enneagram in Love and Work: Understanding Your Intimate & Business Relationships.* San Francisco: Harper San Francisco, 1995.

*Riso, Don Richard and Russ Hudson. *Personality Types: Using the Enneagram for Self- Discovery.* Boston: Houghton-Mifflin, 1996.

* good introductory book   **excellent business reference

*Rohr, Richard with Andreas Ebert. *Discovering the Enneagram: An Ancient Tool for a New Spiritual Journey*. New York: Crossroad, 1990.

Publication

Enneagram Monthly—Annual Subscription $40. Call 518-279-4444.

* good introductory book   **excellent business reference

APPENDIX IV: **SELECTED READINGS—TYPE SPECIFIC**

Type One:

Bender, Sue. *Everyday Sacred: A Woman's Journey Home*. San Francisco: Harper San Francisco, 1996.

Carson, Richard D. *Taming Your Gremlin: A Guide to Enjoying Yourself*. New York: HarperCollins, 1986.

Type Two:

Dass, Ram and Paul Gorman. *How Can I Help?: Stories and Reflections on Service*. New York: Knopf, 1985.

Type Three:

Harrison, Steven. *Doing Nothing: Coming to the End of the Spiritual Search*. New York: J. P. Tarcher, 1998. (audio cassette available from Sounds True, Louisville, CO, 1999.)

Type Four:

Bender, Sue. *Plain and Simple: A Woman's Journey to the Amish*. San Francisco: Harper San Francisco, 1991.

Moore, Thomas. *The Re-enchantment of Everyday Life*. New York: HarperCollins, 1997.

Type Five:

Goleman, Daniel. *Emotional Intelligence: Why It Can Matter More Than IQ*. New York: Bantam Books, 1997.

Kornfield, Jack. *A Path with Heart: A Guide through the Perils and Promises of Spiritual Life*. New York: Bantam Doubleday Dell Publishing Group, 1993.

Type Six:

Rodegast, Pat and Judith Stanton. *Emmanuel's Book: A Manual for Living Comfortably in the Cosmos*. New York: Bantam Books, 1987.

Type Seven:

Chödrön, Pema. *The Wisdom of No Escape and the Path of Loving-Kindness*. Boston: Shambhala Publications, 1991.

Type Eight:

Richards, M. C. *Centering: In Pottery, Poetry, and the Person*. Hanover, N.H.: University Press, 1989.

Type Nine:

Covey, Stephen. *The Seven Habits of Highly Effective People*. New York: Simon & Schuster, 1989.

Type One: *A Clear and Present Danger*. Harrison Ford portrays the One.

Type Two: *When a Man Loves a Woman*. Andy Garcia plays a Two to Meg Ryan's One.

Type Three: *Quiz Show*. Character Van Doren is classic Three.

Type Four: *The French Lieutenant's Woman*. Meryl Streep plays a Four in two time periods.

Type Five: *Awakenings*. Robin Williams portrays a Five physician.

Type Six: *French Kiss*. Meg Ryan plays a phobic Six.

Type Seven: *Mrs. Doubtfire*. Robin Williams plays a Seven who learns sobriety.

Type Eight: *The Fugitive*. Tommy Lee Jones exemplifies Eight energy.

Type Nine: *What's Eating Gilbert Grape?* Johnny Depp is the self-forgetting Nine.

APPENDIX VI: **TELL YOUR OWN STORY**

Tell your own story of using the Enneagram in everyday life. Send it to lynette@everydayenneagram.com. I'll post the best ones on my Web site, so that we all may learn more about practical use of the Enneagram map. (I'll change names and circumstances if you desire.)

Please visit my Web site at www.9points.com. Be sure to click on the globe which will take you to the Gathering Place Bulletin Board, where Enneagram enthusiasts around the world share stories, offer insights, and ask questions of those inhabiting the nine types. We have been building community for Enneagram folks at large. If you feel shy about asking your question on the bulletin board, email me at Lynette@everydayenneagram.com. I'll try to get back to you as soon as I can.

Be sure and check out the Enneagram Store, as well as Lynette's favorite Web sites, where you'll find other Enneagram experts and useful information. If you want to find out more about available books, tapes, etc., click on Books and Resources. If you wish to order, just click on the title and it will take you to that book on Amazon.com. Internet bookstore.

Give the Gift of
The Everyday Enneagram
to Your Friends and Colleagues

CHECK YOUR LEADING BOOKSTORE OR ORDER HERE

❏ **YES,** I want _____ copies of *The Everyday Enneagram* at $25.00 each, plus $5 shipping per book (California residents please add $1.88 sales tax per book).

❏ **YES,** I am interested in having **Lynette Sheppard** speak or give a seminar to my company, association, school, or organization. Please send information.

Please charge my
❏ Visa ❏ MasterCard ❏ Discover ❏ American Express

Name _____

Organization _____

Address _____

City/State/Zip _____

Phone_____ Email _____

Card # _____

Exp. Date_____ Signature _____

Call your credit card order to: 1-800-852-4890
or fax this form to: 707-838-2220

Other inquiries, contact Nine Points Press,
11 La Cresta Drive, Petaluma, CA 94952